English for Journalists

English for Journalists is an invaluable guide not only to the basics of English but to those aspects of writing, such as reporting speech, house style and jargon, that are specific to the language of journalism. Written in an accessible style, beginning with the fundamentals of grammar and the use of English, *English for Journalists* contains a clear summary of the rules of spelling, punctuation and journalistic writing and each point is illustrated with concise examples.

This revised and updated edition includes:

- a discussion of the recent debates surrounding the use of standard and idiomatic English
- a new chapter on the use of arithmetic and figures
- the correct use and spelling of foreign words together with definitions of commonly used Greek and Latin references
- a chapter on broadcast journalism, by Harriett Gilbert, which highlights the problems faced by radio and television journalists
- an updated glossary of journalistic terms and suggestions for further reading

Wynford Hicks is a freelance journalist and editorial trainer. He has worked as a reporter, sub-editor, feature writer, editor and editorial consultant in newspapers, books and magazines, and as a teacher of journalism specialising in the use of English, sub-editing and writing styles. He now lives in France.

English for Journalists

Second edition

Wynford Hicks

London and New York

First published 1993
by Routledge
11 New Fetter Lane, London EC4P 4EE

Simultaneously published in the USA and Canada
by Routledge
29 West 35th Street, New York, NY 10001

Second edition 1998
Reprinted 1999

© 1993, 1998 Wynford Hicks
Chapter 12 © 1998 Harriett Gilbert

Typeset in Goudy Oldstyle by The Florence Group, Stoodleigh,
Devon
Printed and bound in Great Britain by Page Bros (Norwich) Ltd

British Library Cataloguing in Publication Data
A catalogue record for this book is available from the British Library

Library of Congress Cataloguing in Publication Data
Hicks, Wynford
English for journalists/Wynford Hicks. – 2nd ed.
Includes bibliographical references and index.
1. English language–Grammar. 2. Journalism–Style manuals.
I. Title.
PE1112.H53 1998
428.2'024'097–dc21   97–24136

ISBN 0–415–17008–7

Contents

Preface

Since the first edition of *English for Journalists* was published in 1993, controversy has continued about the role of standard English. At its worst this has been an empty conflict between linguistic conservatives who resist all change (often linking it to social decline) and trendy academics who seem to take a perverse delight in undermining the whole idea of 'correctness'.

In her 1996 Reith Lectures, broadcast by the BBC, Jean Aitchison, the Rupert Murdoch Professor of Language and Communication at Oxford University, attacked what she called 'artificially imposed' rules. 'For example', she said, 'an old and illogical belief that logic should govern language has led in English to a ban on the double negative as in "I don't know nothing", which is now standardly "I don't know anything".'

She based her argument on the fact that early English writers such as Chaucer used two or more negatives in place of one as in:

'He *nevere* yet *no* vileyne *ne* sayde
In al his lyf unto *no* maner wight
He was a verray parfit gentil knyght.'

In modern English the double negative can be used in two ways. 'I don't know nothing' is either an assertion of ignorance (non-standard) or the opposite (standard). Quote marks make the second example clearer:

'I don't "know nothing".'

Long before 'rules', artificial or otherwise, were 'imposed' on English the double negative was being used to assert the positive:

'There was *never* anything by the wit of man so well devised, or so sure established, which in continuance of time hath *not* been corrupted.'
(Preface to *The Book of Common Prayer*, 1549, revised 1662)

As with the double negative, so with the double superlative. *The Book of Common Prayer* includes examples of both the single superlative of modern standard English:

> 'That *most excellent* **gift of charity**'
>
> (Collects)

and the (non-standard) double superlative:

> '. . . **counsel of the** *most Highest*'
>
> (Psalms)

Like spelling and punctuation, standard English grammar has become much more regular since the 16th century, as a result of both explicit rule-making and natural evolution. This is what Aitchison elsewhere calls 'neatening up'. As she puts it:

> 'Sweeping up old oddments is good housekeeping, or rather good language-keeping. Gradual neatening up of patterns is inevitable and essential. In this way, the mind avoids becoming overloaded with unpredictable oddments.'

That is precisely why standard English rejects the double superlative and prefers the double negative to have a single function. The argument is about clarity and neatness.

Aitchison's apparent failure to see why the rules of standard English matter is all the more baffling since her function – as she defined it when she became Oxford's Rupert Murdoch Professor – combines research into key aspects of language, especially that of the media, with the education of what she calls 'future lock-keepers', some of whom get work experience on News International newspapers.

In a hostile review of the first Reith lecture the language expert David Crystal criticised Aitchison for ignoring the relationship between speech and writing and asserted:

> 'The point of standard English is that it is essentially a written language phenomenon – chiefly a feature of print. Examine the English newspapers in Sydney, Tokyo, Athens, Atlanta, or Edinburgh, and you will find little difference in their grammar and vocabulary. Standard written English patently exists, as a world-wide medium.'
>
> (*Independent on Sunday*, 11 February 1996)

Crystal added – almost as an afterthought – that the spoken form of standard English was learnt by 'a few people . . . the people most in the national or international public eye – such as broadcasters'.

Clearly, broadcasters do need to pay attention to the way they speak. But what is the relationship between this and the written form of standard English? In what ways do broadcast journalists' problems differ from those of their print colleagues? In this edition of *English for Journalists* a chapter on broadcast journalism by Harriett Gilbert answers these and other questions.

The Crystal position on standard English is an advance on Aitchison's – but it does not go far enough. Indeed it could be described as highly elitist. For when does a prospective broadcaster start to learn the spoken form of standard English? And since some people are brought up to speak it, or at least learn it at school, do they not have a powerful advantage if they decide on a career in broadcast journalism?

A similar argument could be put forward about careers in other areas of public life such as politics, the law, the civil service, the diplomatic service, etc. Since progress in them depends on the ability to master the spoken form of standard English, those who have to learn this after they leave school must be at a disadvantage.

From the social point of view the effect of not teaching spoken, as well as written, standard English to schoolchildren as a matter of course is surely to reinforce middle-class domination of public life. Which, presumably, is the opposite effect of that intended by the opponents of standard English.

Surveys constantly tell us that the British are innumerate as well as illiterate; newspapers are full of mistakes based on poor arithmetic and general confusion about figures. Percentages seem a particular weakness. That is why I have included a short chapter on figures (Chapter 11) in this edition.

Similarly, the section on foreign words has become a chapter in its own right. This is because, as their use increases, the general knowledge of them seems to decline.

Other additions include: an introduction to Chapter 3; a paragraph or two on paragraphing in Chapter 5; a revision of the entry on Americanisms; and the *Times Literary Supplement*'s own hitlist of clichés in Chapter 9.

I have also removed the odd mistake published in the first edition. Please let me know via Routledge if you spot anything wrong in this one.

Wynford Hicks
Libourne, 1997

Acknowledgements

I would like to thank my colleagues – students, trainee journalists and fellow tutors – for their comments and suggestions. Particular thanks to Harold Frayman and Michael Mills for checking the chapters on figures and foreign words respectively.

How to use this book

You can, of course, begin the book at the beginning and read it straight through. It is planned to lead you in logical order from the basic rules of English to suggestions on style and vocabulary.

But if you have a particular interest – for example, in punctuation – turn to the chapter that covers it and read that first. You may come across an unfamiliar term, such as 'preposition': use the index to find out where the term is explained. In fact, it is covered in the chapter 'Grammar: the rules'.

If you want advice on a particular point – for example, use of the word 'hopefully' – instead of reading all the chapters where it might be covered, begin with the index. In fact, 'hopefully' is covered in 'Grammar: mistakes and confusions'.

1
The use of English

English is one of the most flexible and expressive languages in the world. Its immense vocabulary provides for the precise and persuasive communication of ideas. It is a language of subtle verbal inflections, which enable the writer to project mood and emotion, to formulate thought and principle with clarity and impact. It is a language made for, and by, poets, playwrights and philosophers. And it is a reporter's language in which graphic words can be used to tell a story in vivid detail.

But the very richness of English makes it difficult to use well. If there are always so many ways of saying something, how can you be sure you have chosen the right one? For example, should you write in formal English or as you speak? Should you use long, impressive phrases or short, expressive ones? And what about imported words, whether from a foreign language or American?

English began as a combination of Anglo-Saxon and Norman French with a strong dose of Latin, and as it spread, developed a series of dialects – American, Australian, West Indian and so on. Today the strongest influence on the way we speak and write is undoubtedly American. In the global village of satellites and computers it is in American rather than English that nation speaks unto nation.

But that is no reason why we in Britain should say 'off and running' instead of 'up and running', 'around 50' instead of 'about 50', 'meet up with' instead of 'meet' – or why we should 'wash up' before we eat rather than afterwards or start wearing our 'vests' over rather than under our shirts. Above all, we should avoid the ugly American jargon of modern warfare, marketing and computerbabble.

The best advice to a journalist is: write for your reader. You should use a clear form of English, avoiding jargon, slang, pomposity, academic complexity, obscurity . . .

Different publications have different readers so you should apply common sense. A broadsheet newspaper will use longer words than a tabloid; a trade magazine will be more formal than a women's magazine; a specialist computer magazine can hardly avoid some jargon. But the general principles of good writing apply to all publications.

This book takes as a premise that standard English is a useful means of communication, and that it is essential for journalists to learn and remember the rules of grammar, spelling and punctuation. Sub-editors, in particular, must know what it is they are doing – otherwise their intervention in copy is inconsistent, arbitrary and pointless.

Certainly, when you know the rules of grammar, you can, where appropriate, break them: write 'who' for 'whom' in the sentence 'Whom did you invite?'; 'It's me' instead of 'It is I'; 'painters like Picasso' instead of 'painters such as Picasso'. At least then you will know what you are doing and be able to defend it.

But there is never an excuse for sentences like this one (included in a *Guardian* obituary of Lady George-Brown):

> Born of Jewish parents, her husband made much of her race whenever he found himself embroiled in arguments with Israeli politicians or representatives of the Jewish community in Britain.

The grammar of the sentence says that Lord George-Brown was born of Jewish parents – but if he had been, why the need to invoke his wife's 'race'? His own would have done well enough surely. No, the meaning of the sentence must be that it was Lady George-Brown who had the Jewish parents – hence her husband's use of her background for his political purposes.

This mistake – failing to match the subject of an introductory phrase with the subject of the main clause – is made daily in British newspapers and magazines. It is called the dangling modifier (see pp. 13–14).

On vocabulary this book is less prescriptive than some others. It recognises that the meanings of words change with time, and vary between different groups in society. Most people now use the word 'celibate' to mean 'abstaining from sex' rather than 'unmarried', though a Catholic priest's vow of celibacy still refers to marriage rather than sex. Most people now use 'regularly' to mean 'often', though it is also used to mean 'at regular intervals'. Most people now use 'alibi' to mean 'excuse', though for lawyers, police officers and villains it keeps its original meaning of 'being elsewhere when a crime is committed'.

The best advice with such words is to use them with care; if in doubt, find an alternative. Here, as everywhere, your guiding principle must be: what will my reader understand by the words I use?

2
Grammar
The rules

Grammar is the set of rules and conventions that are the basis of the language.

Early English grammars were derived from the rules of Latin. The result was that they were over-rigid and even included 'rules' that did not apply to English at all. For example, there is no rule of English grammar that prohibits split infinitives, or prepositions to end sentences, or conjunctions to start them. These are matters of style not grammar.

In the 1960s English grammar was accused of restricting the personal development and free expression of young people. The previously accepted form of standard English was declared to be both a straitjacket on self-expression and a devious means of keeping the working class and ethnic minorities in their place. The result was that in many politically correct classrooms the teaching of English grammar was virtually abandoned.

But the pendulum has swung back, and learning the rules of grammar is now an important part of the national curriculum. This is surely right – above all, for journalists, who act as interpreters between the sources they use and their readers and listeners. Not to know the grammar of their own language is a big disadvantage for a writer – and a crippling one for a sub-editor.

A comprehensive English grammar would constitute a book of its own. What follows is an attempt to list the main grammatical terms and rules you need to know. The next chapter describes common mistakes and confusions.

Note: the term 'syntax', meaning grammatical structure in sentences, is not used in this book. Instead the general term 'grammar' is used to cover both the parts of speech and the structure of sentences.

THE PARTS OF SPEECH

There are eight parts of speech: noun, pronoun, adjective, verb, adverb, preposition, conjunction and interjection.

NOUN

Nouns are the names of people and things. They are either ordinary nouns called *common* ('thing', 'chair') or special nouns called *proper* ('George', 'Tuesday'). Proper nouns generally take a capital letter.

Abstract common nouns refer to qualities ('beauty', 'honesty'), emotions ('anger', 'pity') or states ('friendship', 'childhood').

In general nouns are *singular* ('thing', 'man') or *plural* ('things', 'men'). But some nouns are the same in the singular and the plural ('aircraft', 'sheep') and some are used only in the plural ('scissors', 'trousers'). Nouns that refer to collections of people and things ('the cabinet', 'the team') are known as *collective* nouns.

PRONOUN

Pronouns stand for nouns and are often used to avoid repetition. They can be:

> *personal* ('I', 'yours', 'him')
> *reflexive/intensive* ('myself', 'herself', 'themselves')
> *relative/interrogative* ('who', 'whose', 'whom')
> *indefinite* ('anybody', 'none', 'each')

The noun that a pronoun stands for is called its *antecedent*.

Pronouns, unlike nouns, often change their form according to the role they play in a sentence: 'I' becomes 'me'; 'you' becomes 'yours'. This role of a noun or pronoun is called *case*. Following the Latin model, grammarians used to talk about such things as the nominative, dative and genitive cases. But this is needlessly complicated: the key distinction is between the *subjective* case ('I') and the *objective* case ('me').

VERB

Verbs express action or a state of being. They are called *finite* because they have a subject ('He thinks') or *non-finite* because they do not ('to think').

Finite verbs

Mood: verbs are either

>*indicative*, that is statement or question ('He sees the ball'/'Does he see the ball?')

>*imperative* ('Go on, hit the ball')

>*subjunctive* ('If he were to see the ball . . .').

Indicative tenses

There are three basic times (present, past, future) and three basic actions (simple, continuing, completed). Thus there are nine basic tenses:

	Simple	*Continuing*	*Completed*
Present	I see	I am seeing	I have seen
Past	I saw	I was seeing	I had seen
Future	I shall see	I shall be seeing	I shall have seen

Three other tenses show a mixture of continuing and completed action:

>Present: I have been seeing
>Past: I had been seeing
>Future: I shall have been seeing

Grammarians traditionally distinguish between the first person singular ('I'), the second person singular ('thou'), the third person singular ('he/she'), the first person plural ('we'), the second person plural ('you') and the third person plural ('they'). But modern English has dispensed with the second person singular ('thou' is archaic), and in most verbs only the third person singular differs from the standard form:

>I see
>He/she sees
>We see
>You see
>They see

Subjunctive tenses

The verb forms for the subjunctive mood are much the same as for the indicative. But there are two exceptions.

The third person singular, present tense, changes as follows:

'She *has* faith' becomes 'If she *have* faith'
'He *finds*' becomes 'Should he *find*'.

The verb 'to be' changes as follows:

Present

Indicative	*Subjunctive* (*if*)
I am	I be
He/she is	He/she be
We are	We be
You are	You be
They are	They be

Past

Indicative	*Subjunctive* (*if*)
I was	I were
He/she was	He/she were

'We were', 'you were' and 'they were' remain unchanged.

Non-finite verbs

There are three types of non-finite verb:

1 the *infinitive* ('to see')
2 the *present participle* ('seeing')
3 the *past participle* ('seen')

Note that 'to' is sometimes omitted from the infinitive. 'I want *to see*' and 'I can't *see*' are both examples of the infinitive.

The participles are used to make up the basic tenses (see above).

The present participle is also used as a noun ('seeing is believing'), as an adjective ('a far-seeing statesman') and in phrases (see *Phrases*, pp. 13–14).

The past participle is also used as an adjective ('an unseen passage') and in phrases.

ADJECTIVE

An adjective describes a noun or pronoun.

The most common adjectives are the *definite article* (the) and the *indefinite article* (a, an).

Demonstrative adjectives (this, that, these, those) identify a noun ('this car', 'these potatoes'). When used without a noun they become pronouns ('This is my car').

Possessive adjectives (my, your, our) show ownership ('my car').

Most other adjectives are *absolute adjectives* (final, perfect) or *adjectives of degree*.

Adjectives of degree are either

> *positive*, used of a thing ('hot', 'complicated')
> *comparative*, used to compare one thing with another ('hotter', 'more complicated')
> *superlative*, used to compare a thing with two or more others ('hottest', 'most complicated')

ADVERB

An adverb usually describes a verb, adjective or other adverb:

> He sees *clearly* [adverb describes verb].
> It was a *newly* minted coin [adverb describes adjective].
> He sees *very* clearly [adverb describes adverb].

Some adverbs are used to link sentences; they are called *sentence adverbs* or *conjunctive adverbs* and are usually marked off by commas:

> Life is expensive. Death, *however*, is cheap.

Note that 'however' can also be used as an ordinary adverb:

> *However* good you may be at punctuation, you will still make mistakes.

PREPOSITION

A preposition is a word that links its object with a preceding word or phrase:

> It's a case *of* mumps.
> We're going *to* Blackpool.

When the object of a preposition is a pronoun it must be in the objective case. Thus:

> *of* me
> *to* her
> *for* him
> *by* us
> *with* them

CONJUNCTION

A conjunction is a word that:

1 links two similar parts of speech

> fit *and* well
> slowly *but* surely

2 links two sentences whether or not they are separated by a full stop

> You may come. *Or* you may go.
> You may come *or* you may go.

3 links main clauses with subordinate clauses and phrases

> I will *if* you will.
> I will go *as* a clown.

INTERJECTION

An interjection is a short exclamation that is outside the main sentence. It either stands alone or is linked to the sentence by a comma:

> *Alas*! Woe is me!
> *Hello*, how are you?

SENTENCES

A sentence is a group of words expressing a complete thought. It has a *subject*, the person or thing being discussed, and a *verb*, expressing action or a state of being (and it may have other elements such as an object):

> *Subject*   *verb*
> The man   sees.

Sometimes the subject is understood rather than stated:

> The old man lay down. And died.

In the second sentence 'he' is understood.

There is also a looser definition of a sentence:

> a piece of writing or speech between two full stops or equivalent pauses
> (*New Shorter Oxford English Dictionary*, 1993)

Sadly, this attempted catch-all fails to include the *first* sentence in a piece.

But a single word can certainly be a sentence:

Agreed.
Indeed.

The first of these consists of a verb with the subject implied; the second can mean the same thing. In each case what makes the word a sentence is that it expresses a complete thought. So the definition we started with holds – with two minor revisions:

A sentence is *a word or group of words* expressing a complete thought and ending with a full stop.

TRANSITIVE VERBS AND OBJECTS

A sentence may have an *object*, the person or thing that receives the action of the verb. This kind of verb is called *transitive*:

Subject	verb	object
The man	sees	the sun.

An object may be *direct* or *indirect*:

Subject	verb	direct object	indirect object
The man	gives	the dog	to his son.

Subject	verb	indirect object	direct object
The man	gives	the dog	a bone.

Note that 'to' is sometimes, but not always, included with an indirect object.

INTRANSITIVE VERBS

If nothing receives the action of the verb it is *intransitive*:

Subject	verb
The man	walks.

If an intransitive verb is followed by something to extend or complete its meaning this is not called an object:

The man walks slowly [adverb].
The man walks to work [adverbial phrase].

ACTIVE AND PASSIVE VERBS

A transitive verb is in the *active voice*. It can also be turned round so that it is in the *passive voice*:

Active
The man sees the sun.
Passive
The sun is seen by the man.

Be careful when you combine the passive with a participle:

The workers were penalised by sending them back.

is incorrect because the subject of both main verb and participle must be the same. Instead write either:

They penalised the workers by sending them back.

or:

The workers were penalised by being sent back.

INACTIVE VERBS AND COMPLEMENTS

If a verb expresses not action but a state of being it is inactive and takes a *complement*.

Subject	*verb*	*complement*
The man	is	ill.
He	feels	a fool.

Note that some verbs can be either transitive or inactive:

He feels ill [complement].
He feels the cloth [object].

Note that both direct and indirect objects are in the objective case but that complements, like their subjects, are in the subjective case:

I see him [object].
I am he [complement].

AGREEMENT OF THE VERB

The verb must agree with its subject in person and number:

I give.

but:

He gives [person].

Spelling is important.

but:

Spelling and grammar are important [number].

1 Note that words joined to a single subject by a preposition do not affect the verb:

> Spelling, with grammar, is important.

2 If two subjects are linked by 'either, or' or 'neither, nor' the verb agrees with the nearer subject:

> Neither the news editor nor any of his reporters have received the call.

3 If one subject is affirmative and the other negative the verb agrees with the affirmative one:

> The chief sub, not her deputies, was at lunch.

4 The verb in a defining clause agrees with its nearer antecedent:

> He was one of the best subs that have ever worked here.

5 Nouns that are plural in form but singular in meaning take a singular verb:

> News is what the reader wants to know.
> Thirty pages is a lot of copy.
> Law and order is a plus for New Labour.

In the last example 'law and order' takes a singular verb because it is a routine combination. If we separate the two elements we need a plural verb:

> 'Law' and 'order' are both nouns.

6 The word 'number' is treated as singular when it is a figure but as plural when it means 'a few':

> A number is stamped on each computer.

but:

> A number of computers are needed.

7 Singular pronouns such as 'everyone' take a singular verb. 'None' can be either singular or plural:

> Are there any bananas? No, there are none.
> Is there any beer? No, there is none.

8 Collective nouns take either a singular or a plural verb according to sense:

> The team is small [it has few players].

but:

The team are small [its players are not big].

The cabinet is determined [it is seen as a single body].

but:

The cabinet are discussing [it takes at least two to discuss].

The cabinet is divided [it must be seen as one before it can be divided].

but:

The cabinet are agreed [it takes more than one to agree].

Do not mix the two forms. Do not write:

The cabinet is divided but they are discussing . . .

Note that many house-style books insist on organisations being treated as singular. If this is your style, follow it.

SENTENCE STRUCTURE

A sentence with only one verb is a *simple* sentence:

The man sees the sun.

A sentence with two or more main verbs is a *compound* sentence:

The man sees the sun and he closes his eyes.

A sentence with one or more main verbs and one or more subsidiary verbs is a *complex* sentence:

The man who sees the sun closes his eyes.

☆ CLAUSES

A clause is a group of words including a subject and a verb forming part of a sentence. A compound sentence has two or more main clauses; a complex sentence has at least one main clause and at least one subordinate clause. In the sentence above the main clause is 'The man closes his eyes' and the subordinate clause is 'who sees the sun'.

A distinction must be made between clauses that define and those that do not. Consider the sentence above with and without commas:

The man who sees the sun closes his eyes [in general a man who sees the sun will close his eyes].
The man, who sees the sun, closes his eyes [this particular man, having seen the sun, closes his eyes].

With things you can make the distinction clear by using 'that' to define and 'which' in a non-restrictive way:

> This is the house that Jack built [clause defines the house].
> Fred's house, which was built in 1937, is up for sale [clause does not restrict, adds incidental information].

With people, too, 'that' can be used to define:

> This is the man that I told you about.

But 'which' cannot be used of people.

So where the clause defines, use 'that' (or 'who' of people) and do not use commas; where the clause does not define, use 'which' (or 'who' of people) and include commas.

A final test is: can you omit the subordinate clause altogether without making the main clause meaningless? If you can, always use 'which' (or 'who') of people and include commas.

PHRASES

A phrase is a group of words without a verb forming part of a sentence.

An adjectival phrase must be related to the correct noun or pronoun.

> A readable book, it has a good index.
> *Correct*: the phrase 'a readable book' describes the subject 'it'.

> A readable book, its value is enhanced by a good index.
> *Incorrect*: the phrase 'a readable book' cannot describe the subject 'its value'.

> Like Belfast, Beirut has known civil war.
> *Correct*: the phrase 'like Belfast' describes the subject 'Beirut'.

> Unlike Belfast, bomb blasts no longer echo across the city.
> *Incorrect*: the phrase 'unlike Belfast' cannot describe the subject 'bomb blasts'.

This mistake is called the dangling modifier. A particularly common example of it is the dangling, floating or hanging participle:

> Walking across the road, he was run over by a car.
> *Correct*: the phrase 'walking across the road' describes the subject 'he'.

> Walking across the road, a car ran him over.
> *Incorrect*: the phrase 'walking across the road' cannot describe the subject 'a car'.

The mistake is so common that sometimes it seems hardly noticeable. But it may be ludicrous:

> When dipped in melted butter one truly deserves the food of the gods.

Or it may be ambiguous:

> 'Far worse, after having a child killed, police have deceived Mr and Mrs Bridgewater.'

The person quoted here (one of the Bridgewater Four, freed after 18 years in jail) is not accusing the police of conspiracy to murder, only of deceit: it is the Bridgewaters whose son Carl has been murdered – that is, they have suffered twice.

3
Grammar
Mistakes and confusions

People, including journalists, make grammatical mistakes for all sorts of reasons – ignorance, haste, carelessness. This is obvious. But why should national broadsheet papers such as the *Times, Independent* and *Guardian* print so many howlers?

One reason is that computers make it possible for the sub-editing process to be streamlined – which is a euphemism for 'done away with'. Nowadays writers are clearly responsible for most of the mistakes published in broadsheet newspapers.

The craft of subbing has survived better in the tabloid papers than in broadsheets. This helps to explain why Harry Blamires in his study of bad journalistic English (*Correcting Your English*, Bloomsbury, 1996) said he found that the tabloids were 'not a fruitful source of material'.

A second reason for the problem is that sentences in broadsheets are often long and complex. And it is a fact about language that such sentences are more likely to have mistakes in them.

So check your copy even more carefully when you find it necessary to write a long and complex sentence such as this one taken from the *Guardian*:

> The investigation was prompted by a *Sunday Times* story – hotly denied by one of the businessmen involved – claiming a donation from a British-based Serbian entrepreneur had been made of 'less than £100,000' and was regarded as so sensitive that it was reported to security services, the Cabinet office and Mr Major.

Was it the investigation, the story or the donation that was 'regarded as so sensitive'? If it was the donation the change of tense from 'had been made' to 'was reported' confuses the issue – and so does the trendy omission of 'that' after 'claiming'. Does the cash figure matter (why *less than* £100,000?) and how many businessmen/entrepreneurs were there?

It's difficult to know where to stop. Simple subbing could tidy the sentence up a bit – but, on second thoughts, perhaps it would be wiser to start again.

On the other hand, it may be the urge to be brief and punchy that gives us fragments – such words as 'while', 'because' and 'since' starting subordinate clauses pretending to be sentences. The habit is more common in tabloids than in broadsheets. Here, for example, is the *Daily Mail's* star columnist Lynda Lee-Potter in typical jerky, attention-grabbing style:

> Lee wasn't a lager lout or a work-shy layabout. He was a conscientious, ambitious boy with a loving family; and his needless tragedy is a warning to us all.

> Because drink has become our culture, it's an integral part of everyday life. In the Fifties . . .

No, it doesn't mean what it appears to mean: that drink has become our culture and *so* is an integral part of everyday life. Instead the word 'because' is intended to refer to the previous paragraph: the tragedy is 'because' of drink.

But here 'because' means nothing – take it away (also the 'it's' after the comma) and the sentence becomes stronger as well as more grammatical:

> Drink has become our culture, an integral part of everyday life.

Even if people talk in these fragments it is a mistake to write like this because it is confusing: readers expect sentences starting with 'because' to end with a main clause.

In other cases, a lively defence of loose grammar can be made on the grounds that it is sanctioned by popular usage, particularly in speech. 'Different to' is far more common than 'different from'; 'compare to' is far more common than 'compare with' when 'with' is correct; 'the media' and other plurals are often treated as singulars; 'which' is confused with 'that' and 'due to' treated as indistinguishable from 'owing to', etc.

Grammar does not stand still. In the past 30 years the plural pronoun 'they/them' has replaced the singular:

> If anybody comes let them in.

So the next edition of this book may have to take a different view of some of the examples given below. But for the moment the best advice is not to make what are still considered mistakes. And above all try to be clear. That will help you avoid such sentences as this one:

> They are clever, they are determined, they are ambitious and some do have a different approach to men . . .

The writer meant 'a different approach from that of men' – but you have to work it out.

A AND AN

Words with a silent 'h' such as 'honest' take 'an' instead of 'a':

> an honest man

Unless your style book directs, do not extend this to such words as 'hotel' and 'historian'.

ABSOLUTE ADJECTIVES

Do not misuse absolute adjectives such as

absolute	ideal
basic	impossible
complete	obvious
empty	perfect
essential	pure
fatal	ultimate
final	unique
full	

A thing is either perfect or less than perfect. It cannot be 'more perfect' or 'most perfect'. It is similarly ludicrous to write 'more fatal' or 'more unique'.

AND AND BUT

See *Conjunctions to start sentences*, pp. 19–20.

AND WHICH

Do not write 'and which' unless it follows 'which'. For example, do not write:

> The incomes policy, announced last week by the government *and which* aims to control inflation, is supported by the opposition.

Avoid similar misuses of 'and that', 'but which', etc.

AS GOOD AS

If 'as good as' is followed by 'if not better than', do not omit the second 'as':

> He is as good, if not better, than I am.

Either write:

> He is as good as, if not better than, I am.

or, better:

> He is as good as I am, if not better.

BETWEEN AND AMONG

Use 'between' of two people or things; 'among' of three or more people or things. But also use 'between' to show a relationship between one person/thing and several others:

> There is no love lost between my brothers and me.

BETWEEN/AND

'Between' must be followed by 'and'. Do not write 'between 1914–18'. Write either 'in 1914–18' or 'between 1914 and 1918'.

BOTH

See *Saying it twice*, p. 26.

CENTRE AROUND, IN AND ON

See *Prepositions: the pitfalls*, p. 25.

COMPARE LIKE WITH LIKE

Be careful to compare like with like. Do not write:

> Fred's efforts were better than Jim.
> France's exports were worth more than Italy.

COMPARE TO AND WITH

Use 'with' for routine comparisons – like with like, last year's figures with this year's. Use 'to' when the comparison itself makes a point as in:

> Shall I compare thee to a summer's day?

COMPRISE (OF)

See *Prepositions: the pitfalls*, p. 25.

CONJUNCTIONS TO START SENTENCES

There is no problem with the use of 'and' and 'but' to start sentences. Whatever your English teacher may have said to the contrary, this practice is not a grammatical mistake.

Nor is it a grammatical mistake to write:

> Because the food was awful they walked out.

But it is usually stronger to put the 'what' before the 'why':

> They walked out because the food was awful.

Subordinate clauses starting with conjunctions such as 'because', 'while' and 'though' should not be used as stand-alone sentences as in:

> They walked out. Because the food was awful.
> They walked out. Though they had paid for the meal in advance.

The point is that here – and almost everywhere – the reader expects a sentence starting with 'because', 'while' or 'though' to have a main clause.

You can sometimes get away with the device by preparing the reader for it:

> Why did they walk out? Because the food was awful.

But don't overdo it.

DANGLING MODIFIERS

See Chapter 2, *Grammar: the rules*, pp. 13–14.

DIFFERENT FROM, THAN AND TO

See *Prepositions: the pitfalls*, p. 25.

DOUBLE NEGATIVE

In modern standard English the double negative asserts the positive rather than emphasising the negative. Thus:

> I don't know nothing.

can mean that the speaker knows something rather than nothing:

> I don't 'know nothing'.

But in many people's speech it means the opposite. So beware of using the double negative in copy since it may be misunderstood.

DUE TO

'Due' is an adjective and is also used in adjectival phrases:

> The rent is *due*.
> The cancellation is *due to bad weather*.

Strict grammarians – and many house-style books – say that 'due to' may not be used to introduce an adverbial phrase; that what follows is a mistake:

> The train was cancelled *due to bad weather*.

So the best advice, whatever British Rail may say, is: don't do it.

EQUALLY

See *Saying it twice*, p. 26.

FEWER AND LESS

Distinguish between 'fewer', which refers to number, and 'less', which refers to volume:

> *Fewer* strawberries in the fields results in *less* fruit in the shops.
> If there are *fewer* trees there will be *less* wood.

Above all, do not write 'less' of people as in:

> Less people know grammar nowadays.

Note the difference between:

> The less people know about it the better.

and:

> The fewer people know about it the better.

FLOATING, HANGING PARTICIPLES

See Chapter 2, *Grammar: the rules*, pp. 13–14.

FOLLOWING

'Following' (originally a participle) is often used by journalists as a preposition to mean either 'after' or 'because of', as in:

> Following the rain the sun came out (after).
> The M4 is still closed following a pile-up (because of).

But it can be ambiguous as in:

> Following the success of New Labour in Britain, the French left hopes to do well in the elections.

Is there really a connexion here or is the journalist trying to link two unrelated events in the reader's mind?

Be clear: instead of 'following' use either 'after' or 'because of'.

FOR YOU AND I

Avoid being posh – and wrong at the same time. The preposition 'for', like all the rest, must be followed by the objective case: always write 'for me' not 'for I'.

FROM/TO

'From' must be followed by 'to'. Do not write 'from 1939–45'. Write either 'in 1939–45' or 'from 1939 to 1945'.

HOPEFULLY

Expressions such as 'hopefully' and 'generally speaking', although they are, strictly speaking, 'dangling modifiers' (see Chapter 2, *Grammar: the rules*, pp. 13–14), are increasingly accepted in everyday journalism.

But avoid imprecision. In 'Generally speaking, grammar is important' and 'Hopefully, your punctuation will improve' the speaker/writer expresses an opinion, but it is not clear who shares it. Where it is important to be precise, always write:

> *I* hope your punctuation will improve.

or:

> Let *us* hope your punctuation will improve.

LAY AND LIE

Do not confuse 'lay' and 'lie' as many Americans do, particularly in pop songs. 'Lay' is a transitive verb and so takes an object; 'lie' is an intransitive verb and does not:

> Chickens *lay* eggs.
> Waiters *lay* the table.
> Soldiers *lay down* their arms.

but:

> A sun-worshipper *lies down* on the beach.

LIKE AND SUCH AS

Do not confuse 'like' and 'such as'. 'Like' makes a comparison; 'such as' introduces examples:

> Fruit trees, like flowers, need water.
> Fruit trees such as the plum and the cherry need pruning.

If you write 'Fruit trees like the plum and the cherry . . .' you imply that the plum and cherry are not fruit trees.

MAY AND MIGHT

Do not confuse 'may' and 'might': they are different tenses of the same verb.

'First aid may have saved him' suggests that he had first aid and we do not yet know whether he will survive.

'First aid might have saved him' suggests that he did not have first aid but if he had, it is possible that he would have survived.

MEET

Do not use 'with' (still less 'up with') when 'meet' means 'come face to face with' (a person):

> Fred met Joan at the station.

Use 'with' when 'meet' means 'chance to experience' as in:

> He met with an accident.

MYSELF

The pronoun 'myself' has two uses.

> I sub myself.

is either reflexive, meaning:

> I sub my own copy.

or intensive – that is, it emphasises:

> I too am a sub-editor.

'Myself' should not be used in place of 'me' in such sentences as:

> They asked Fred and me to work on the story.

NO QUESTION

Be careful with this phrase and its variants, such as 'no argument'. A TV producer once wrote to the *Observer* to complain that he had been quoted as saying:

> 'The four are outspoken and there is no question we encouraged them to play up for the camera.'

As he went on:

> What does this damaging ambiguity mean – that we did or that we didn't?

To convey the TV producer's meaning the quote should have read:

> 'There *was* no question *of our encouraging* them . . .'

A *Guardian* reporter once wrote:

> There is no argument that the Rev Lucy Winkett, aged 29, is talented and highly intelligent.

The reporter wanted to emphasise Lucy's wit and talent but succeeded only in calling it into question. To convey her meaning accurately she could have written:

> There is no argument but that . . .

But it would have been far simpler and clearer to write:

> There is no *doubt* that . . .

ONE AND YOU

Do not mix the two impersonal pronouns 'one' and 'you'. Either write:

> If one wants to be a journalist, one should learn to use one's eyes.

or, better:

> If you want to be a journalist, you should learn to use your eyes.

Do not write:

> If one wants to be a journalist, you should learn to use your eyes.

In general use 'you': leave the formal 'one' to the royal family.

ONLY

Be careful with 'only': putting this word in the wrong place can affect the meaning of a sentence.

'I'm only here for the beer' is unlikely to be misunderstood, but what is meant by 'He only eats here on Tuesdays'? That on Tuesdays he refrains from drinking? Or that he eats here only on Tuesdays?

To be clear, put 'only' directly before the word or phrase it refers to.

PREPOSITIONS: THE PITFALLS

The most common mistake is to use the wrong preposition or to use one where it is not necessary. Note the following examples of commonly misused prepositions:

acquiesce *in* (not *to*)
affinity *between, with* (not *to, for*)
agree *on* (a point), *to* (a proposal), *with* (a person or opinion)
alien *from* (not *to*)
arise *from* (not *out of*)
bored *with* (not *of*)
capacity *for* (not *of*)
centre *on/in* (not *around*)
compare: see p. 19
comprise: no preposition (do not use *of*)
consider: no preposition (do not use *as*)
correspond *with* (a person), *to* (a thing)
credit *with* (not *for*)
die *of* (not *from*)
differ *from* (in comparisons, not *to* or *than*), *with* (a person
    when disagreeing)
different *from* (not *to* or *than*)
dissent *from* (not *to*)
fed up *with* (not *of*)
glad *at* (a piece of news), *of* (a possession)
impatient *for* (a thing), *with* (a person)
independent *of* (not *from*)
indifferent *to*
martyr *for* (a cause), *to* (a disease)
meet: see p. 23
oblivious *of* (not *from* or *to*)
part *from* (a person), *with* (a thing)
prefer *to* (not *than* or *rather than*)
prevail *against* (a thing), *on* (a person)
prevent *from*
protest *at/against*
reconcile *to* (a thing), *with* (a person)
taste *of* (food), *for* (the arts and other things)

Most compound prepositions are an abomination. Avoid such expressions as:

in connection with
in regard to
in relation to

PREPOSITIONS TO END SENTENCES

Ending a sentence with a preposition may sometimes be bad style but it is not bad grammar. As Winston Churchill once wrote (defending his own writing from redrafting by a pedantic civil servant): 'This is the sort of English up with which I will not put.'

So, where your ear tells you that a preposition can go at the end of the sentence, put it there.

SAYING IT TWICE

Beware of tautology – saying things twice. In the examples below the word underlined is superfluous – and makes the sentence illiterate.

> He is <u>equally</u> as good as gold.
> John and Mary were <u>both</u> talking to each other.
> They were restricted to <u>only</u> one drink.
> The crowd was estimated at <u>about</u> 1,000.
> <u>It is possible</u> she may come to the party.

The same error is made in this example:

> The reason people steal is <u>because</u> they need the money.

This should be either:

> People steal because they need the money.

or:

> The reason people steal is <u>that</u> they need the money.

See also *Redundant words* p. 78.

SINCE

Be careful with 'since' which can mean both 'because' and 'from the time that'. The following sentence is at best confusing, at worst nonsensical:

> They were the wrong gender since they were children.

It is intended to mean:

> They have/had been the wrong gender since they were children.

SPLIT INFINITIVE

'To boldly go' is a split infinitive: the infinitive is divided by an adverb. It is often bad style but it is not bad grammar.

In deciding whether or not to split the infinitive ask yourself:

1 Is the adverb superfluous? Often it contributes nothing to the sense.
2 Would the adverb be better somewhere else in the sentence?
3 Would the sentence sound better/make better sense if it were rewritten?

If the answer to these questions is no, split away.

SUPERLATIVES

Do not use the superlative where you should use the comparative. For example, you cannot have 'the least of two evils' or 'the best of two games' or 'the eldest of two brothers'. And do not use a double superlative such as 'most fondest'.

If you qualify a superlative, as in 'the world's second longest river', be careful. The sentence 'The Amazon is the world's second longest river after the Nile' needs at least a comma after 'river' (brackets are better). Otherwise it means that the Amazon is the world's *third* longest river.

To put it another way, without a comma it would be more exact to write:

The Amazon is the world's longest river after the Nile.

THAT AND WHICH

See Chapter 2, *Grammar: the rules*, p. 13.

TRY TO/AND

After 'try' use the infinitive form not a conjunction. Write 'try *to* write' not 'try *and* write'.

WHO AND WHOM

Most people say and write 'Who did you invite to dinner?' although the correct form is 'Whom did you invite?'

Increasingly the informal, 'incorrect' form is acceptable.

Some journalists who wish to be formal write:

>   *Whom* **did you say came to dinner?**

This is a mistake, since 'whom' here is the subject of the sentence: it should be '*Who* did you say came to dinner?'

WITH

Just as the preposition 'with' does not affect the verb in:

>   **Spelling, with grammar, is important.**

so it does not affect the subject in:

>   **With her husband she faced the press.**

Do not write:

>   **With her husband they faced the press.**

4
Spelling

English spelling often defies logic. Why should we spell 'harass' with one 'r' and 'embarrass' with two? Why does 'mantelpiece' echo its Latin origin (*mantellum*, cloak) while 'mantle', the posh word for 'cloak', does not? Why does 'dependent' (the adjective) differ from 'dependant' (the noun)?

Whereas punctuation evolves, spelling does not. Whereas with grammar and punctuation you can sometimes argue a case for loose, colloquial usage, with spelling there is no way out. The word is either right or wrong – though some words are spelt in more than one way (see Chapter 7, *House style*, pp. 56–8).

Nobody expects you to know how to spell all the words in the dictionary. The key thing is to avoid mistakes: learn to recognise the words you cannot spell and look them up.

WORDS PEOPLE GET WRONG

First, here's a list of words that many people can't spell. Get somebody to test you on it.

abhorrence	benefited
accidentally	blamable
accommodation	braggadocio
acquiescence	bureaucracy
admissible	
annihilate	Caribbean
apartment	clamouring
apostasy	connoisseur
asinine	consensus
asphyxiate	convertible
authoritative	corpuscle
auxiliary	corroborate

crucifixion

debatable
definitely
descendant
desiccated
destructible
diagrammatic
diarrhoea
dignitary
discernible
dispel
dissatisfaction
dysentery

ecstasy
effervescence
eligibility
embarrass
emissary
exaggerate
exhilaration
expatriate

fallacious
forty
fulfilling
funereal

gaseous
guttural

haemorrhage
harass
heinous
herbaceous
hiccup
hierarchy
humorous
hygiene
hysterical

ideologist
idiosyncrasy
impresario
indispensable
indissoluble
innocuous

innuendo
inoculate
instalment
intestacy
iridescence

jeopardise

kitchenette

liaison
licentious
linchpin
liquefy
loquacious

maintenance
manoeuvre
mantelpiece
mayonnaise
meanness
Mediterranean
mellifluous
millennium
miniature
minuscule
miscellaneous
mischievous
moccasin

negotiate
nonchalant
noticeable

obeisance
occurred
omitted
oscillate

paraphernalia
pavilion
perspicacious
plummeted
predilection
privilege
profession
proprietary
pseudonym

publicly
pursue
Pyrenees

rarefy
recommend
reconnaissance
referred
restaurateur
resuscitate
riveted

sacrilegious
separate
statutory
straitjacket

supersede

targeted
tranquility

unforeseen
unnecessary
unparalleled

vacillate
verruca
veterinary
vociferous

withhold

CONFUSIONS

(See also Chapter 9, *Words*, pp. 75–7.)

One reason why people misspell some words is that they confuse them with other words. There are three common kinds of confusion:

1 a word is confused with a shorter one that sounds the same

coconut	cocoa
consensus	census
dispel	spell
fulfil	full/fill
minuscule	mini
playwright	write
supersede	cede

2 a word is confused with a different one that sounds the same

altar	alter
aural	oral
bail	bale
bait	bate
born	borne
breach	breech
cannon	canon
complement	compliment
cord	chord
counsel	council
curb	kerb
currant	current
deserts (runs away/ what is deserved)	desserts (puddings)

draft	draught
discreet	discrete
expatriate	ex-patriot
faze	phase
forbear	forebear
forego	forgo
foreword	forward
formally	formerly
geezer	geyser
grisly	grizzly
hanger	hangar
horde	hoard
lead (the metal)	led (the past participle)
lightening	lightning
metal	mettle
principal	principle
raise	raze
review	revue
sight	site
stationary	stationery
storey	story
swat	swot
toe	tow
way	weigh
yoke	yolk

3 a word used as one part of speech is confused with the same word used as another part of speech

Noun	Verb
practice	practise, *so also* practising, practised
licence	license, *so also* licensing, licensed
envelope	envelop, *so also* enveloping, enveloped.

Noun	Adjective
dependant	dependent

In one of the pairs listed above the words are pronounced differently:

Noun	Verb
*en*velope	en*vel*op

If you find it difficult to distinguish between the common pairs *practic(s)e* and *licenc(s)e*, note that *advic(s)e* changes its pronunciation as well as spelling and remember the three pairs together:

Noun	Verb
advice	advise
practice	practise
licence .	license

or remember the sentence:

> Doctors need a licence to practise.

In this case the noun ('c') comes before the verb ('s').

Also note the opposite problem: two words with the same spelling that are pronounced differently and have different meanings:

*in*valid (as in chair)	in*valid* (as in argument)
de*serts* (runs away, what is deserved)	*de*serts (sand)
lead (the metal)	lead (the present tense)
re*ject* (verb)	*re*ject (noun)
pro*ject* (verb)	*pro*ject (noun)

I BEFORE E

Most people know the spelling rule 'i' before 'e' except after 'c'. This gives:

> believe, niece, siege

and

> ceiling, deceive, receive

But note that the rule applies only to the 'ee' sound and that there are exceptions such as:

> caffeine, codeine, counterfeit, protein, seize

and, in the other direction:

> species

PLURALS

1 Nouns ending in a consonant followed by 'y' take 'ies' in the plural:

lady	ladies
penny	pennies
story	stories

But proper nouns take the standard 's' in the plural:

> the two Germanys
> three Hail Marys
> four Pennys in a class list

And nouns ending in a vowel followed by 'y' take the standard 's' in the plural:

donkey   donkeys
monkey   monkeys
storey   storeys

2 Most nouns ending in 'o' take the standard 's' but some common ones take 'es' in the plural:

buffaloes, cargoes, dingoes, dominoes, echoes, embargoes, goes, heroes, mangoes, mottoes, negroes, noes, potatoes, tomatoes, tornadoes, torpedoes, vetoes, volcanoes

And some may be spelt either with 's' or 'es':

archipelago, banjo, grotto, halo, innuendo, memento, mosquito, salvo

3 Nouns ending in 'f' usually take the standard 's' in the plural:

dwarf   dwarfs
handkerchief   handkerchiefs

(although 'dwarves' and 'handkerchieves' are found).

But note:

elf   elves

4 Some nouns that come from Greek, Latin or modern languages keep their original plural form:

addendum   addenda
alumna   alumnae
alumnus   alumni
bacillus   bacilli
chateau   chateaux
criterion   criteria
minimum   minima
phenomenon   phenomena
spectrum   spectra

In some cases both the original plural form and an anglicised version are used:

appendix	appendices (used of books)	appendixes (used of both books and the body)
beau	beaux	beaus
bureau	bureaux	bureaus
cactus	cacti	cactuses
formula	formulae (scientific)	formulas (general use)

fungus	fungi	funguses
index	indices (mathematics)	indexes (books)
medium	media (the press, etc.)	mediums (spiritualism)
memorandum	memoranda	memorandums
plateau	plateaux	plateaus
stadium	stadia	stadiums
syllabus	syllabi	syllabuses
terminus	termini	terminuses
virtuoso	virtuosi	virtuosos

Be careful of confusing the singular with the plural when the latter form is more common as with:

graffito	graffiti
die	dice
stratum	strata

The plural of 'wagon-lit' is 'wagons-lits', not as some British dictionaries insist 'wagons-lit' or 'wagon-lits'; the plural of 'court martial' is 'courts martial'.

But note that plurals such as 'agenda', 'data' and 'media' are often treated as though they were singular. Check your house style.

SUFFIXES

1 One-syllable words with a short vowel and a single final consonant double it before a suffix that starts with a vowel.

| fat | fatten, fatter |
| run | runner, running |

2 So, too, do words with more than one syllable if the stress is on the final syllable.

begin	beginning, beginner
refer	referred, referral
prefer	preferred – but note *prefer*able (pronounced *pre*ferable)

3 But one-syllable words with a long vowel or double vowel do not double the final consonant.

| seat | seated, seating |
| look | looking, looked |

4 Nor do words with more than one syllable if the stress is before the final syllable.

*proff*er   proffering, profferred
*bene*fit   benefiting, benefited
*leaf*let   leafleting, leafleter

5 Exceptions to these rules include most words ending in 'l':

cavil   cavilling
devil   devilled (but *devilish*)
level   levelled
revel   reveller
travel   traveller

but:

parallel   paralleled

and some words ending in 'p' or 's':

worship   worshipped
bus   buses
gas   gases

while some words ending in 's' are optional:

bias   biased or biassed
focus   focused or focussed.

House style determines whether the extra 's' is added.

6 Sometimes the stress changes when a noun is used as a verb:

format   formative but for*mat*ted (in computer speak)

Dictionaries generally give:

combat   combatant   combative   combated

But there is an argument for 'combatted' on the grounds that some people pronounce it that way. (You can, of course, avoid the problem altogether by using 'fight' as a verb instead of 'combat': it's one character shorter.)

7 Whether 'learn' becomes 'learnt' or 'learned', 'dream' becomes 'dreamt' or 'dreamed', is a matter of house style. But 'earn' can only become 'earned'.

8 Words ending in a silent 'e' keep it if the suffix begins with a consonant:

safe   safety
same   sameness

But note that there are common exceptions:

due	duty
true	truly
awe	awful (but awesome)
wide	width

And some words are optional:

acknowledg(e)ment, judg(e)ment

9 Words ending in a silent 'e' drop it if the suffix begins with a vowel:

bake	baking
sane	sanity

but:

change	changeable
mile	mileage

Note that 'y' here acts as a vowel:

gore	gory
ice	icy

10 Sometimes keeping or losing the silent 'e' makes it possible to distinguish two words with different meanings:

dying (the death)	dyeing (clothes)
linage (payment by the line)	lineage (descent)
singing (musically)	singeing (burning)
swinging (from a tree)	swingeing (heavy)

AGREEMENT

A few words taken from French have an extra 'e' for the feminine form:

blond(e), brunet(te), confidant(e), débutant(e).

Note that in French an adjective agrees with its noun not the person the adjective refers to. Thus (since hair has no gender in English):

A blonde woman has blond hair.

This logical point is made in several house-style books – but generally ignored.

'Chaperon(e)' is a curiosity. In French *chaperon* exists only as a masculine noun; in English the (false) feminine form 'chaperone' is far more common.

5
Punctuation

The point of punctuation is to make your writing easier to read. It is the counterpart of the pauses and inflections that make speech understandable. But be careful: it does not necessarily follow that everywhere you would pause in speech you should punctuate in writing. And sometimes the strength of a punctuation mark differs from the length of the equivalent pause in speech.

Ideally, punctuation should be based on sound logical principles. But be careful: do not try to force your punctuation practice into a format that defies current usage.

One modern school of thought says: the less punctuation the better. And it is certainly true that there is less punctuation than there used to be, for all sorts of reasons: sentences are shorter so they need fewer intermediate stops; as abbreviations become familiar they no longer need to be marked as such; designers dislike dots . . . But be careful: don't be ultra-modern or you risk confusing your reader.

THE FOUR MAIN STOPS

These are: the comma, the semicolon, the colon and the full stop. Of these the comma is the weakest and the full stop the strongest with the colon and semicolon somewhere in between. Some books still say that the colon is a stronger stop than the semicolon – and it can be – but it isn't always stronger. It makes more sense to say that the semicolon lies midway between a comma and a full stop while the colon now has a series of specialist uses.

COMMA

1 Use the comma to separate a series of words of the same kind:

The reporter should always write clear, concise, accurate English.

but do not use the comma when a series of adjectives is cumulative:

He ordered a rich chocolate sponge cake.

Note that there is usually no comma before the 'and' at the end of a list of single words:

She said the same to James, Stephen, Mark and John.

2 Use the comma to separate a series of phrases of the same kind:

His writing was more refined, more intellectual, more Latinate, than Smith's.

Use a comma before the 'and' at the end of a list where it helps to prevent confusion:

They invited Charles and Mary, Andrew and Susan, and Anne.

3 Use the comma to mark off words that address somebody or something:

Come on, City.

4 Use the comma, where appropriate, to mark off words or phrases such as 'however', 'for example', 'in fact', 'of course':

With punctuation, however, it pays to be careful.

Note that many journalists now omit the comma in most such cases – but you should always include it if there is any chance of misunderstanding.

5 Use the comma to mark off a word in parenthesis:

Born in Little Rock, Arkansas, he went to Washington.

6 Use the comma to mark off a phrase in parenthesis:

Norman Mailer's first novel, *The Naked and the Dead*, was a bestseller.

Do not use the comma where the phrase is essential to the meaning of the sentence:

Norman Mailer's novel *The Naked and the Dead* was a bestseller.

Note that in this example commas would mean that Mailer had written only one novel.

Also note the difference between 'the Home Secretary, Michael Howard,' and 'Michael Howard, the Home Secretary,' (both parenthetical, so commas) and 'Home Secretary Michael Howard' and 'the Tory MP Michael Howard' (not parenthetical, so no commas).

7 Use the comma to mark off a clause in parenthesis:

> The paper's subs, who were in their shirt sleeves, worked fast.

Do not use the comma where the clause is essential to the meaning of the sentence:

> The subs who were in their shirt sleeves worked fast; those
> who were wearing summer dresses worked even faster.

But note the example below which breaks this rule:

> He who can, does. He who cannot, teaches.

8 Use the comma, where necessary, to mark off an introductory phrase or clause:

> Because of the appalling weather, conditions for holidaymakers
> were described as 'intolerable'.

Where a phrase or clause that needs commas follows a conjunction such as 'but' or 'and', the first comma is now considered to be optional:

> Fred tried to get up but (,) because he was tired and
> emotional, he failed.

9 Use the comma, where two sentences are joined by a conjunction, if you want to lengthen the pause:

> He wanted to leave the party, but his friend detained him.

Do not use the comma where the subject of the two sentences is the same:

> He wanted to leave but didn't.

Do not use the comma between sentences where there is no conjunction: Avoid:

> He wanted to leave, his friend detained him.

But note the example below of a series of short sentences where the comma can be used:

> I came, I saw, I conquered.

SEMICOLON

1 Use the semicolon between sentences, with or without a conjunction, as a longer pause than a comma and a shorter one than a full stop:

> The rumour was that the king was dead; the people believed it.
> There will be an inquest, of course; but the matter will not end there.

2 Use the semicolon to separate longer items in a list, particularly if the items themselves need further punctuation by commas:

> Punctuation marks include the full stop, which is the strongest stop; the semicolon, which is weaker; and the comma, which is weakest of all.

COLON

1 Use the colon, in preference to the comma, to introduce full-sentence quotes:

> He said: 'Punctuation is difficult.'

2 Use the colon to introduce lists:

> All of them were dead: Bill, Jack, Ted and Willie.

3 Use the colon between two sentences where the second explains or justifies the first:

> Keep your language uncluttered: it reads more easily.

4 Use the colon between two sentences to mark an antithesis:

> Man proposes: God disposes.

5 Use the colon in a caption to connect the person or object in the picture with the rest of the caption:

> Napoleon: 'Victory is ours'
> Victorious: Napoleon

FULL STOP (FULL POINT, PERIOD)

Use the full stop in text to mark the end of a sentence. You do not need to use full stops after headlines, standfirsts, captions and other forms of displayed type: remember that white space punctuates. See Chapter 7, *House style*, pp. 56–8, on the use of full stops after initials and abbreviations.

THE PARAGRAPH BREAK

The paragraph break can be called the fifth main stop since it is one stage stronger than the full stop. As with other forms of punctuation its main purpose is to make reading easier. A new paragraph can signal a change of subject or give the reader a rest.

Journalism is inclined to use short pars because it is typeset in columns of a few words to the line (rather than across the page as in this book), so that a given number of words looks longer on the page. And journalists write knowing that they need to struggle to catch and keep the reader's attention.

The shorter the par the more it stands out.

Tabloids use shorter pars than broadsheets since they have narrower columns and fight harder for the reader's attention. News stories are written in shorter pars than features because they are less of a read, more of a series of facts. They assume a reader in a hurry with a short attention span.

Commentators from outside journalism sometimes criticise its short pars for producing a jerky, disjointed effect. But they miss the point that in news writing this is part of the style.

A news intro in both tabloids and broadsheets is usually a stand-alone sentence written to give the gist of the story.

After the intro the story starts all over again and is told in greater detail, with each stage having a new par. When you have written your intro, the best guide to structuring a news story is to answer your reader's questions in the order you think they would ask them.

In many news stories disparate elements are brought together; each one needs its own par.

The reporter and the news sub are not expected to manipulate the material so that the copy gains an artificial smoothness. In news – as in life – there are often abrupt entrances and loose ends left lying around.

A feature, by contrast, should flow. Each par should be written to follow the one before so that the reader is seduced into continuing to read whatever their interest in the content. Thus a feature often has bridges linking one par with another and its pars are usually longer than those in news.

But the occasional short one can have a dramatic effect.

It is hard to give general advice about how long (or short) your pars should be. But:

- If your news intro goes beyond 25 words you should think again and try to rewrite it.
- In news a par that goes beyond three sentences/10 lines is likely to be too long.
- Never quote two people in the same par: always start a new one for the second quote.
- Never tack a new subject on to the end of a par.
- In features avoid a succession of short pars – unless you want to produce a jerky effect.

QUOTATION MARKS (QUOTE MARKS, QUOTES)

1 Use quote marks for direct speech: see Chapter 6, *Reporting speech*, pp. 51–3.

2 Use quote marks for extracts from written reports, following the same rules as for speech.

3 Use quote marks in a headline to show that an assertion is made by somebody in the story rather than by your publication: this can be vital in court stories.

4 Whether you use double or single quotes in text is a matter of house style, but in headlines always use single quotes.

5 For quotes within quotes use double inside single, and vice versa:

> He said: 'I really meant to say, "I'm sorry."'
> He said: "I really meant to say, 'I'm sorry.'"

Note that a comma rather than a colon introduces the second quote.

6 Quote marks are sometimes used for the titles of books, plays, etc. – check your house style.

7 Quote marks are sometimes used to emphasise or draw attention to particular words or phrases, to identify slang or technical expressions.

Do not do this unless it is essential for clarity.

Avoid:

> That double-glazing salesman is a 'cowboy'.

Either use slang because it fits the context or find another expression.

8 Whether you use single or double quote marks, be consistent. Do not use one form for quoting people and another for book titles and other uses (see Chapter 7, *House style*, pp. 56–8).

PARENTHESES

1 For a routine, weak parenthesis use commas (see above, pp. 39–40).

2 To mark a strong but unemphatic parenthesis, usually to explain rather than comment, use round brackets (confusingly they are often called 'parentheses'):

> the National Union of Mineworkers (NUM)
> five miles (about eight kilometres)
> Don't call a noisy meeting a shambles (the word means 'slaughterhouse').

When a parenthesis forms part of a sentence, the full stop comes after the second bracket (as here). (But when the whole sentence is a parenthesis, as here, the full stop comes before the second bracket.)

3 To mark a parenthesis that is added by the writer or editor either to explain or comment, use square brackets:

> The novelist writes: 'He [the main character] dies in the end.'
> 'The standard of your spelling and grammer [sic] is terrible.'

4 To mark a strong, emphatic parenthesis, usually to comment rather than explain, use dashes:

> John Smith – the man's a fool – is staying here.

5 The mark that guides the reader to a footnote can be used in journalism.*

OTHER MARKS

DASH

1 Use dashes to mark a strong parenthesis (see above).

2 Use the dash, where appropriate, to introduce an explanation or to sum up:

* But don't overdo it.

Journalism has many forms – newspaper, periodical, broadcast.

Note that the colon here would do as well – the dash is less formal.

Newspaper, periodical, TV and radio – these are the main
forms of journalism.

3 Use the dash to add emphasis or mark a surprise:

This is the point – there's no escaping it.
You'll never guess who wrote the story – Fred Bloggs.

4 Use the dash to mark a change of direction or interruption, particularly in speech:

'I suppose – but what's the use of supposing?'
'I suppose –' 'Why are you always supposing?'

5 Use either the em (long) dash or the en (short) dash, according to
house style.

6 Do not confuse the dash with the hyphen (see below).

HYPHEN

1 Use the hyphen for figures written out:

ninety-nine

2 Use the hyphen, where appropriate, for compound words such as:

(a) titles:

vice-president

(b) prefix plus adjective:

extra-marital sex

The sex takes place outside marriage. By contrast 'extra marital sex'
suggests married couples working overtime.

(c) adjective plus adjective:

red-hot coals

The first adjective modifies the second.

(d) adverb plus adjective used before the noun:

a well-known fact

But note:

The fact is well known.

Also note that there is no need for a hyphen after adverbs ending in '-ly'. So either write:

a close-knit band of men

or:

a closely knit band of men

(e) adjective plus noun:

a black-cab driver

This refers to the driver of a black (licensed) taxi. By contrast 'black cab driver' may suggest that the driver is black.

(f) noun plus noun:

a black cab-driver

This makes it clear that the driver, rather than the cab, is black.

(g) noun plus preposition plus noun:

mother-in-law

(h) verb plus preposition used as noun:

get-together

But note that when used as a verb, the word does not take the hyphen:

We get together at a get-together.

(i) prefix plus proper noun or adjective:

pre-Christian

(j) prefix plus word to distinguish between meanings:

re-creation (*making something again*) recreation (*leisure*)

(k) two words that together make a clumsy or ugly juxtaposition:

supra-intestinal

Caithness-shire

3 Use the hyphen to mark word breaks at the ends of lines. Note:

(a) with unjustified setting (no right-hand margins) hyphens are less common

(b) avoid a succession of word breaks

(c) when you hyphenate, try to break words into their constituent parts

(d) avoid making unintentional words such as *anal-ysis*.

Problem

Double compounds: should it be 'a Jimmy Greaves-type goal', a 'Jimmy-Greaves-type goal' or 'a Jimmy Greaves type goal'?

Solution: Use the first formula unless there is a risk of misunderstanding; then turn the expression round to avoid using the hyphen.

APOSTROPHE

1 Use the apostrophe to show that something is left out of a word:

> don't
> fo'c's'le

Do not use the apostrophe to show that a word has been shortened.

Avoid:

> thro', 'phone, the '60s

Either use the word in full ('through') or in its shortened form without the apostrophe ('phone').

2 Use the apostrophe to mark the possessive:

> women's liberation, lamb's liver, for goodness' sake

This use is extended to cover 'for' as well as 'of'.

The phrase 'children's books' means 'books written for children' at least as often as it does 'books owned by children'.

3 Use the apostrophe *where necessary* to make a plural clear:

> do's and don'ts

This is easier to read than 'dos and don'ts', although the second is increasingly common.

> Mind your p's and q's.

But do not use the apostrophe for routine abbreviations.

Avoid:

> Tom's 40p

Instead of the price of tomatoes, it looks like Tom's pocket money.

Common apostrophe mistakes

1 Putting it in where it doesn't belong, for example, 'everything in it's place', 'Apostrophe's are hard to use.'

2 Leaving it out when it's essential, for example, 'womens liberation', 'Its a fact.'

3 Putting it in the wrong place, for example, 'womens' liberation', 'the peoples' choice'.

Apostrophe problems

1 Place names: 'King's Langley' *but* 'Kings Norton'.

Solution: follow usage and use reference books.

2 Names of organisations: 'Harrods' but 'Christie's'.

Solution: follow the organisation's own style (check the phone directory) unless it is illiterate: do not write 'womens'.

3 The extra 's': 'Thomas' ' or 'Thomas's'?

Solution: follow sound – if the extra 's' is sounded, as it is in:

   St Thomas's

include it; if it is not, as in:

   Jesus' disciples

leave it out.

4 The double apostrophe:

   Fred's book's title

Solution: avoid it where possible; prefer:

   the title of Fred's book

5 The apostrophe with a title in quotes:

   the point of 'Ode to Autumn's' imagery

Solution: avoid – either don't use quotes for titles or write:

   the point of the imagery of 'Ode to Autumn'

QUESTION MARK (QUERY)

Use the query after a direct question:

> Are you coming?
> He asked: 'Are you coming?'

The query is inside the quote marks because the whole question is quoted:

> Have you read 'Ode to Autumn'?

The query is outside the quote marks because the question is not part of the quote.

> Why is everybody always picking on me?

Although the question may be rhetorical – no answer is expected – it still needs a query.

Common query mistakes

1 Including a query in indirect speech:

> He asked if I was coming?

2 Misplacing the query in direct quotes:

> He asked: 'Are you coming'?

EXCLAMATION MARK (SCREAMER)

Use the screamer only when it is essential to mark an exclamation:

> Ooh, I say!

Do not use the screamer to make comments, signal jokes or mark rhetorical questions.

DOTS (ELLIPSIS, LEADER DOTS . . .)

1 Use three dots to show that something has been omitted, for example from a written quotation. But when you edit quotes in writing up an interview, there is no need to use the dots each time you omit a word.

2 Use three dots to mark a pause:

> I suppose . . . but what's the use of supposing?

3 Use three dots to lead the reader from one headline to another when they are linked:

> Not only . . .
> . . . but also

4 Use dots in charts and tables to make them more readable.

OBLIQUE (/)

Use the oblique to mean either, as in 'and/or'.

ASTERISK (*)

Use the asterisk (rarely) for footnotes and, in papers where this is style, to avoid printing a swear word in full – f*** (see *Four-letter words*, p. 74).

BLOB (BULLET POINT ●)

Use the blob either to emphasise items in a list or to mark that a separate story has been added to the main piece.

6
Reporting speech

Reporting speech accurately and clearly is an essential journalistic skill. You must be able to handle both direct quotes and indirectly reported speech.

DIRECT QUOTES

1 When you quote a person for the first time, introduce them before the quote:

> John Smith, the leader of the council, said: 'Of course, I refuse to resign.'

Note that because the quote is a complete sentence, it is introduced by a colon, it starts with a capital letter and the full stop comes before the second quote mark.

2 Subject to house style you can use 'says' instead of 'said':

> John Smith, the leader of the council, says: 'I refuse to resign.'

3 Subject to house style you can use the short form 'council leader':

> Council leader John Smith says: 'I refuse to resign.'

But note:

(a) the style works best when the description is short, say, up to three words: 'company managing director John Smith' is acceptable; 'chairman and managing director John Smith' is probably too long

(b) since the style is supposed to be short and snappy, avoid prepositions such as 'of': 'leader of the council John Smith' is nonsense

(c) since the short description functions as a title, it does not combine well with a real title: 'council leader Dr John Smith' looks and sounds awful and should be avoided.

4 Later in the story variation is possible. Either:

> He said: 'I have done nothing wrong.'

or:

> 'I have done nothing wrong,' he said.

Note that because the quote is a complete sentence, the comma comes before the second quote mark, replacing the full stop in the original.

5 Where the quote is longer than a sentence, put 'he said' either before the quote or after the first complete sentence, not at the end of the quote:

> 'I'm baffled by the accusations,' he said. 'In fact, I can't see what all the fuss is about.'

6 In features, but not in news, you may break the sentence for effect:

> 'I'm baffled,' he said, shaking his head, 'by the accusations.'

7 Where a quote continues for more than a paragraph, repeat the quote marks before each new quoted paragraph:

> 'I'm baffled by the accusations,' he said. 'In fact, I can't see what all the fuss is about.
>
> 'I really don't know what to do about the terrible mess I seem to be in.'

Note that there are no closing quote marks after the word 'about'.

8 In general avoid inverting 'Smith' and 'said'. Never write:

> Said Smith: 'I will never resign.'

An acceptable use of inversion is where 'Smith' follows the quote and in turn is followed by an explanatory phrase or clause:

> 'I will never resign,' said Smith, who has been leader of the council for 10 years.

9 You may want to quote a particular word or phrase:

> He described himself as 'really baffled'.

Note that here, because the quote is not a complete sentence, the full stop comes after the quote mark.

A word of warning: don't litter your copy with bitty quotes; in general try to quote complete sentences.

10 For quotes within quotes use double quote marks inside single and vice versa:

He said: 'I really meant to say, "I'm sorry."'
He said: "I really meant to say, 'I'm sorry.'"

Note that in both cases a comma rather than a colon introduces the second, enclosed quote.

11 Use a new paragraph when you quote a person for the first time.

REPORTED SPEECH

1 The traditional way of reporting speech indirectly is to move most tenses one stage back. Thus the direct quote 'I support electoral reform' becomes:

He said he supported electoral reform.

'I have always supported electoral reform' becomes:

He said he had always supported electoral reform.

'I will always support electoral reform' becomes:

He said he would always support electoral reform.

With the simple past there is usually no change. 'I supported electoral reform until I became leader of the party' becomes:

He said he supported electoral reform until he became leader
of the party.
(But it is possible to put 'had' before 'supported' for clarity/emphasis.)

This traditional style has the clear advantage that succeeding paragraphs in the appropriate tense are clearly identified as reported speech:

He said he started supporting electoral reform as a student
and did so until he became leader of the party.

Whatever anybody else said, he was still committed to change.

Always follow the correct sequence of tenses: 'is/has' becomes 'was/had'.

2 Journalists increasingly use 'he says' instead of 'he said' for reported speech, even in news stories. Thus 'I support electoral reform' becomes:

He says he supports electoral reform.

'I supported electoral reform until I became leader of the party' becomes:

He says he supported electoral reform until he became leader
of the party.

Subject to house style you can use this form – but remember that 'he said' must be used in reporting set-piece events such as speeches, public meetings, courts and tribunals.

3 An advantage of 'he says' over 'he said' is that there is no difficulty in distinguishing between the present 'I support electoral reform' and the past 'I supported electoral reform': the tense remains the same in reported speech. But if you have to use 'he said', it is better to be clear and clumsy than ambiguous. So, where there is the risk of misunderstanding, write:

> He said he supports electoral reform.

4 Unless there is a good reason, do not mix your tenses. Do not write 'he said' in one sentence and 'he thinks' in the next.

5 Do not write: 'Speaking at the meeting the speaker said . . .' Instead write:

> The speaker told the meeting . . .

6 Do not follow the fashion of always leaving 'that' out. Leave it out where the subject remains the same:

> He says he supports electoral reform.

Where the subject changes 'that' is optional:

> He says (that) his opponent supports electoral reform.

But leave 'that' in after words such as 'claims' and 'admits' that have another meaning. Avoid:

> He claims the prize of electoral reform is worth fighting for.

7 Also, be careful with punctuation. As it stands, the sentence 'John Smith admitted Fred Brown wanted to hit him and did so' could mean several different things:

> (a) John Smith admitted that Fred Brown wanted to hit him and that he did so.
> (b) John Smith, admitted Fred Brown, wanted to hit him and did so.
> (c) John Smith admitted [let in] Fred Brown, wanted to hit him – and did so.

GENERAL POINTS

1 In general, where speakers say things that are nonsensical, obscure or ambiguous, report their words indirectly, telling the reader what they intended to say. For example, do not use 'refute' to mean 'deny' since many people think that to refute an argument is to show that it is false. So if a director says 'I refute your claim that my company is corrupt', write:

> The director denied that his company was corrupt.

2 Do not be afraid of repeating 'he says' or 'he said' in your story. The reader is far more likely to be irritated by awkward variants such as 'commented', 'remarked' and 'stated'. Above all, be careful with 'claimed', 'asserted' (negative) and 'pointed out', 'explained' (positive). Use them only where they are accurate and add weight or colour to the story.

3 Avoid adverbs such as 'wryly' to signal jokes. Do not write:

> John Smith describes himself wryly as a plain man in a million.

If the joke is good enough, the reader will not need to be nudged; if it is not, the nudging makes the joke fall flatter.

7
House style

House style is the way a newspaper or magazine chooses to publish in matters of detail. Is 'realise' spelt this way or with a 'z' – and should 'spelt' be 'spelled'? How is the date written, '4 July 1776' or 'July 4 1776', and should there be a comma in the middle? Is it 'Second World War' or 'second world war' or 'World War Two' or 'World War II'? Which courtesy titles (Mr, Mrs, Miss, Ms) should be used and when? What about quote marks: single or double? And so on.

The argument for consistency is very simple. Variation that has no purpose is distracting. By keeping a consistent style in matters of detail a publication encourages readers to concentrate on *what* its writers are saying. And, of course, if there is to be a consistent style, it should be a good one.

It follows that writers and sub-editors need to know the publication's house style. The usual way of ensuring this is by means of a style book issued to staff journalists and sometimes regular freelances.

WHAT THE STYLE BOOK SHOULD COVER

Common headings in newspaper and periodical style books include:

Abbreviations
Accents (on foreign words)
Americanisms
Broadcasting
Capitals or lower case
Captions
Collective nouns (singular or plural)
Courtesy titles
Courts and legal terms

Dates
Figures
Foreign words, names and places
Government and politics
Honours, decorations, etc.
Hyphens
Initials
Italics
Jargon
Measures (including weights)
Military
Naval and shipping
Police and crime
Race (see below)
RAF and aviation
Religion
Royal family, peerage, etc.
Service ranks and their abbreviations
Spelling (for example, 'ageing/aging', 'gaol/jail', 'realise/realize', 'spelled/spelt')
Sport
Titles of books, films, etc.
Trade names
Universities and colleges

Specialist magazines will of course cover their own fields.

A style book should always specify a particular dictionary to be consulted on points it does not cover. The *Oxford Dictionary for Writers and Editors* is often used for this purpose.

Many style books also give guidance on general points of good English and writing style; also typesetting instructions for sub-editors.

RACISM AND SEXISM

Many style books advise: report people's race only when it is relevant to the story. Guidance is often given on when to use 'black' (of a person's skin colour as opposed to 'Black' or 'Asian' or 'negro' or 'coloured').

Some style books also advise against such words as 'businessman' (prefer 'business executive'), 'foreman' (prefer 'supervisor') and 'policeman' (prefer 'police officer'). Certainly, if both men and women are covered by the reference, it is a mistake to use the male suffix '-man' (it is a mistake partly because many readers will be offended by it). But there is no consensus in journalism about how far this process should go: some publications enthusiastically adopt such words as 'chairperson' and 'spokesperson'; others would always avoid them on the grounds that they are awkward and ugly.

Opposition to sexism is also one reason for the widespread adoption of the plural pronoun 'they/them' in place of 'he/him':

If anybody comes let them in.

This is both easy to say and politically correct: it is now the accepted form in most British journalism.

But opposition to sexism is also responsible for the 'Ms' complication. To avoid having to call people 'Miss' or 'Mrs' anti-sexists use the American import 'Ms' – which gives us three rival courtesy titles to choose from. A better bet surely would be to do without such titles altogether: this is already the style of many publications.

FALSE DISTINCTIONS

Style books can go too far, drawing distinctions that turn out to be false. For example, some try to distinguish between double quotes for speech and single quotes for emphasis; or between 'judgment' spelt one way for a legal decision and 'judgement' spelt another way for an ordinary opinion; or between 'inquiry' for an official investigation and 'enquiry' for an ordinary question.

This sort of thing doesn't work because it conflicts with usage: most publications use either double or single quotes for both quotation and emphasis, and use the same spelling for different uses of a word.

Occasionally, usage does make the distinction: the American (and original English) 'program' is used of computers while the French 'programme' is used of TV, concerts and everything else.

8
Style

Style differs from grammar in that it cannot be quantified: it has no precise rules. Style is concerned not so much with the mechanics of language as with the way the writer uses it to play on the sensations of the reader. Style adds impact to writing, strengthens the contact with the reader and heightens their awareness. This is true even though the reader may be unaware of what is happening and unable to analyse the techniques used.

To be effective, a journalist must develop a style that has four principal attributes: suitability, simplicity, precision and poise.

SUITABILITY

The way a story is written must match the subject, the mood and pace of the events described and, above all, the needs of the reader. The style must arouse their interest and maintain it throughout. It must also present the facts or arguments in a way that enables the reader to understand them quickly and easily. For example:

1 If the subject is serious, treat it seriously.
2 If the subject is light, treat it lightly – for example, use a delayed-drop intro or a punning headline.
3 Whatever the subject, do not needlessly offend the reader. Thus, where a story concerns eccentric beliefs or practices, avoid cynicism and facetiousness.
4 Where a story concerns events that have action and movement, the style should suggest pace. Write tersely; avoid superfluous adjectives and adverbs; use direct, active verbs; construct crisp, taut sentences.
5 Where a story concerns a sequence of events, a straightforward narrative style may be the best bet. If you use one event to create impact

in the intro, remember to repeat the reference in its proper time context. Also, make sure your tenses are consistent.

6 Where a story concerns stark, horrific events, avoid the temptation to overwrite. The events themselve will provide all the impact you need.

7 Whatever the story, don't rhapsodise. Remember that understatement is usually more effective than overstatement.

SIMPLICITY

Be direct: get to the point. For example:

1 Prefer the short, Anglo-Saxon word to the long, Latinate one.
2 Prefer the concrete statement to the abstract one.
3 Prefer the direct statement to any form of circumlocution.
4 Avoid words or phrases that merely sound good.
5 Avoid pomposity at all costs.
6 Remember that a sentence must have at least one verb – and that this is its most important word.
7 In general, use transitive verbs in the active voice:

   Jones told the meeting he was resigning.

8 Choose adjectives with care and don't use too many. Avoid tautology: 'a *new* innovation'.
9 In general, prefer the short sentence to the long one, particularly in the intro.
10 Avoid over-complex sentences full of subordinate clauses and phrases.

PRECISION

Precision is vital to the journalist, above all in news reporting. To be precise you need to know exactly what words mean. Study words and their meanings and never use a word you are not sure about. Read Chapter 9, *Words*, carefully and then refer to it when necessary.

You must also master the principles of grammar to ensure that you express your meaning clearly and accurately. Read the chapters on grammar carefully and then refer to them when necessary.

As a writer, do not leave it to the sub to spot inaccuracy or ambiguity. Read your own copy and ask: 'Do I mean what I say and have I said what I mean?' Often the honest answer will be: 'No.'

If you pass that self-imposed test, ask: 'So what?' Often you will find that the story does not go far enough in saying what happens next. Remember that the reader needs to know precisely what is happening.

As a sub, always check when you rewrite that you haven't introduced new errors into the copy. And be careful when you write news headlines to fit. If your first effort is the wrong length, you will try to substitute one word for another. But a synonym must be exact or it may change the meaning of the headline. Always ask yourself finally: 'Does the headline tell the story?' If the answer is 'No', it will need further rewriting.

Also, be careful with verbs where the active and passive voice take the same form:

PEER OWED £20,000

This is ambiguous: was he owed the money or did he owe it?

POISE

Poise is the essence of style: it gives writing balance, ease of manner and lack of strain. Individual words should fit the context. Sentences should be a pleasure to read because they are balanced and rhythmical. Paragraphs should be written to convey the writer's meaning and leave the reader in no doubt that they have grasped it.

With the best prose the reader remains unconscious of technique: they simply enjoy reading the passage. The hard work should all be done by the writer (with a bit of polish by the sub).

Study the section on stylistic devices that follows. Practise using them where appropriate. But, above all, look for good models in journalism and writing generally. If a piece of prose excites you, study it, analyse it – even imitate it. Do not be too proud to copy other writers' tricks.

STYLISTIC DEVICES

Most of the stylistic devices that follow are called tropes or figures of speech. There is no reason why you should learn the names of the more obscure ones, such as synecdoche or metonymy. But the curious thing is that we take both of these for granted. What could be more natural than to say 'All hands on deck' (synecdoche) or 'He is a lover of the bottle' (metonymy)? But it is worth remembering that they are in fact figures of speech.

ALLITERATION

Alliteration is the repetition of an initial sound in words that follow each other:

> Sing a song of sixpence

Use in light-hearted stories, particularly in headlines. Do not use in serious stories.

ASSONANCE

Assonance is the repetition of a vowel sound in words that follow each other:

> The cat sat on my lap.

Use in light-hearted stories, particularly in headlines. Do not use in serious stories.

GRAVEYARD (ALSO BLACK, GALLOWS, SICK) HUMOUR

This is making jokes about such things as injury, disease, disability and death. It is an understandable reaction by journalists (also police officers, soldiers, doctors, nurses and others) to the hard facts of life and death.

Enjoy the jokes but do not let them get into print. The headline 'Hot under the cholera' once appeared over a story about an epidemic. This is also an example of the compulsive pun.

HYPERBOLE

Hyperbole is extravagant and obvious exaggeration:

> a million thanks

Of all figures of speech, hyperbole is the most used – and abused – by journalists. So the message must be: handle with care.

IRONY

Irony is either making a point in words that literally mean the opposite or a condition in which a person seems mocked by fate or the facts.

A story about a woman who survives a car crash, borrows a mobile phone and telephones her husband to report her survival – only to be knocked down and killed a moment later – is an example of irony.

In this example telling the story is enough: we do not need to be reminded that it is irony.

Use the word 'irony' sparingly. In particular, avoid the adverb 'ironically' which is usually a lazy way of trying to make a surprise sound more significant than it is.

LITOTES

Litotes is the opposite of hyperbole. It is understatement, especially assertion by negation of the contrary. Instead of 'Rome is a great city':

> **Rome is no mean city.**

METAPHOR

Metaphor is calling something by the name of what it resembles:

> **To suffer the slings and arrows of outrageous fortune**

Frequent repetition of metaphors turns them into clichés (see Chapter 9, *Words*). Careless use of metaphors can lead to the mixed metaphor, an expression in which two or more metaphors are confused:

> **to take arms against a sea of troubles**
> (you wouldn't use *weapons* to fight the *waves*)

The fact that Shakespeare did it is no defence: Hamlet was mad. So avoid the mixed metaphor at all costs since it has the opposite effect of that intended. Instead of making your prose vivid it produces the effect of absurdity.

METONYMY

Metonymy is replacing the name of something by the name of a related thing:

He is a lover of the bottle [instead of drink].

ONOMATOPOEIA

Onomatopoeia is using words whose sound helps to suggest the meaning:

He has a hacking cough.

OXYMORON

Oxymoron is combining contradictory terms to form an expressive phrase:

He shows cruel kindness.

PUN

A pun is a play on words alike or nearly alike in sound but different in meaning:

ALL THE FAX ABOUT NEW TECHNOLOGY

The pun is overused by headline-writers who can't break the habit. *Never* use a pun over a serious story.

A subtler form of word play recycles an old meaning:

ARE YOU A VIRGIN ABOUT OLIVE OIL?

REPETITION

Repetition on purpose emphasises:

O Romeo, Romeo! Wherefore art thou Romeo?

In general, prefer repetition to variation.

RHETORIC

Rhetoric is a general term for the art of using language to persuade or impress others. Note particularly the rhetorical question that journalists address to their readers:

Have you ever been to China?

Use in chatty features, but rarely elsewhere.

SIMILE

Simile is likening something to something else:

My love is like a red, red rose

Frequent repetition of similes turns them into clichés (see Chapter 9, *Words*) – avoid this like the plague.

SYNECDOCHE

Synecdoche is using the part for the whole or the whole for the part:

All hands on deck.

VARIATION

Variation is using a different word or phrase to describe something in order to avoid repetition and/or to add colour to the copy. When done to impress it is called 'elegant variation':

Instead of talking about a *spade* I shall from now on refer to a *horticultural implement.*

This kind of variation is a bad idea because what results is at least strained and sometimes ludicrous.

More common is the variation that tries to avoid repetition:

Northern Ireland has a higher rate of unemployment than at any other time in *the province's* history.

Before using this kind of variation ask yourself the following questions:

1 Would a pronoun do as well? In the example above 'its' could easily replace 'the province's'.
2 Is the variation word/phrase an exact equivalent? (Here the province of Ulster has three counties in the Irish Republic.)
3 Is the variation necessary or could you avoid it by rewriting the sentence?
4 Would repetition have as much impact as variation?

The need to repeat or vary words is often a clue to bad structure. For example, where an intro doubles back on itself, it should be rewritten. Where you are tempted to use 'however' because you have just used 'but', you are making the reader work too hard.

9
Words

Precision and effectiveness in writing depend on the careful use of language. You must learn to recognise the words and phrases that will convey your meaning exactly and vividly to the reader. And you must reject any word or phrase that is flabby and worn out.

The development of word power comes only with practice. Besides a sensitivity to language it demands an inquiring mind and a careful attitude. You must avoid careless mistakes and also be concerned about quality, taking professional pride in your skill as a writer.

This attitude cannot be taught, only caught. But it is worth pointing out common pitfalls.

EXAGGERATION

Many errors occur because the writer overstates the case in an effort to achieve impact: this is perhaps the journalist's most common fault. It is this striving for effect that makes every rescuer 'a hero', every disturbance a 'fracas', every confusion a 'chaos' and every fire an 'inferno' (the word means hell).

Here the advice must be: never use a word whose meaning you are unsure about; always check the dictionary definition and derivation of an unfamiliar word.

TABLOIDESE

The search for a short word to use in a headline has created a specialised subs' vocabulary that, on some papers, turns every investigation into a 'probe', every attempt into a 'bid' and every disagreement into a 'row'. It would be perverse to object to the use of these words in headlines, although a succession of them reads like parody. A sub who writes:

VICE VICAR TELLS ALL IN PROBE BID ROW

is clearly overdoing it.

The real problem comes when this essentially made-up language creeps into the text. Such words as 'rap', 'slam' and 'axe' litter the pages of the downmarket tabloids. As Keith Waterhouse has pointed out, the objection to these words is that people don't use them in everyday speech.

> Why, if these words are now so common, are they not in common use? Why do we not hear housewives at bus-stops saying ... 'Did I tell you about young Fred being rapped after he slammed his boss? He thinks he's going to be axed'?
> (Keith Waterhouse, *Waterhouse on Newspaper Style*, Viking, 1989 pp. 229–30)

So think hard before using the following words in text:

aid	for (help)
aim	(intend)
alert	(tell)
axe	(sack)
ban	(prohibit, exclude)
bar	(exclude)
battle	(dispute)
bid	(try, attempt)
blast	(criticise)
blaze	(fire)
blitz	(drive)
blow	(disappointment)
blunder	(mistake)
bombshell	(unexpected event)
boob	(mistake, breast)
boost	(encourage, increase)
boot out	(expel)
brand	(describe)
bungle	(mistake)
call	(propose)
chief	(leader)
clampdown	(control)
clash	(dispute)
condemn	(criticise)
crackdown	(control)
crusade	(campaign)
curb	(restrict)
curse	(bad luck)

dash	(hurry)
deal	(agreement, arrangement)
don	(put on)
drama	(event)
dramatic	(unusual)
dub	(describe)
dump	(sack)
dwell	(live)
epic	(very unusual)
face	(expect)
feud	(quarrel)
fury	(anger)
grab	(take)
headache	(problem)
hike	(increase)
hit out	(criticise)
hurdle	(difficulty)
inferno	(fire)
jinx	(bad luck)
kick out	(expel)
launch	(start)
loom	(threaten)
mercy	(relief)
oust	(replace)
outrage	(anger)
peace	(end to dispute)
plan	(proposal)
pledge	(promise)
plunge	(fall)
poised	(ready)
probe	(inquiry)
quit	(resign)
quiz	(question)
race	(hurry)
rally	(support)

rap	(tell off)
rebel	(person disagreeing)
riddle	(mystery)
rock	(shock)
romp	(sex, have sex)
row	(dispute)
rumpus	(dispute)
scrap	(cancel)
set to	(likely to)
shake-up	(reform)
shock	(surprise)
shun	(avoid)
slam	(criticise)
slap	(impose)
slash	(reduce)
snag	(difficulty)
snub	(fail to attend)
soar	(increase)
storm out	(resign)
swoop	(raid)
threat	(possibility)
unveil	(announce)
vice	(sex)
vigil	(patrol)
vow	(promise)
war	(rivalry)

POSH WORDS

Posh, pompous, pretentious words are the opposite of tabloidese: they show the writer putting on collar and tie to impress. Many posh words used in journalism are also examples of circumlocution (long-winded and roundabout writing) or euphemism (using a mild-sounding alternative word to avoid giving offence). In general, prefer plain words to posh ones. For example, avoid:

a large proportion of	use (much of)
accede to	(allow, grant)
accommodate	(hold)
accordingly	(so)
additionally	(also)
address	(face, approach)

adjacent to	(near, next to)
ameliorate	(improve)
amidst	(amid)
amongst	(among)
approximately	(about)
ascertain	(learn)
assist/ance	(help)
at an early date	(soon)
at present/at the present time	(now)
attempt	(try)
beverage	(drink)
commence	(begin, start)
concept	(idea)
concerning	(about)
construct	(build, make)
converse	(talk)
customary	(usual)
deceased	(dead)
demise	(death)
demonstrate	(show)
dentures	(false teeth)
despite	(although)
discontinue	(stop)
dispatch	(send)
donate	(give)
draw to the attention of	(point out)
dwell	(live)
edifice	(building)
endeavour	(try)
eventuate	(happen)
evince	(show)
exceedingly	(very)
expedite	(hurry)
extremely	(very)
facilitate	(ease, help)
finalise	(complete)
following	(after)
frequently	(often)
give rise to	(cause)
implement	(carry out)
in addition	(also)

in addition to	(as well as)
in attendance	(present)
in conjunction with	(and)
in consequence of	(because)
indicate	(show, point, point out, say, imply)
in excess of	(more than)
inform	(tell)
initiate	(begin, start)
in order to	(to)
inquire	(ask)
in short supply	(scarce)
in spite of the fact that	(although)
in the course of	(during)
in the event of	(if)
in the neighbourhood/vicinity of	(near)
in the region of	(about)
in view of the fact that	(since)
less expensive	(cheaper)
locate	(find)
location	(place)
made good their escape	(escaped)
manufacture	(make)
missive	(letter)
necessitate	(compel)
nevertheless	(but)
nonetheless	(but)
objective	(aim)
of the order of	(about)
on the part of	(by)
owing to the fact that	(because)
pass away/over/to the other side	(die)
personnel	(workers)
previous	(earlier)
prior to	(before)
proceed	(go)
purchase	(buy)
regarding	(about)
remunerate	(pay)
require	(need)
residence	(home)

resuscitate	(revive)
somewhat	(rather)
subsequently	(later)
sufficient	(enough)
terminate	(end)
to date	(so far)
transportation	(transport)
upon	(on)
utilise	(use)
venue	(place)
was of the opinion that	(thought)
was suffering from	(had)
when and if	(if)
whilst	(while)
with the exception of	(except)

The word 'dwell' contrives to be both tabloidese and posh: a double reason for not using it. The word 'indicate' is a particular trap: does it mean show, point, point out, say or imply? If it's precision you want, avoid 'indicate' altogether. Envelopes are addressed, and golf balls, but not problems – except by the pretentious.

VOGUE WORDS

Some (usually long) words become fashionable. Suddenly they are every-where – used with meaningless frequency by journalists who are keen to be considered smart or who are too idle to develop their own vocabulary.

Using a phrase such as 'the eponymous protagonist' to describe Hamlet is almost always a sign of showing off. So take care with the following:

agenda	dichotomy
ambience	dilemma
ambivalent	
archetypal	egregious
axiomatic	emotive
	empathy
cachet	eponymous
catalyst	escalate
charisma	exponential
conceptual	
coterie	iconic

insulate	replete
meaningful	seminal
meritocracy	symbiosis
milieu	syndrome
mores	
	technocrat
parameter	
pragmatism	vertiginous
protagonist	viable
purposive	vicarious

If you are tempted to use one of these words ask yourself:

1 Is it the exact word you need?
2 Is there an alternative that would be as accurate – and more comprehensible?
3 If not, can the word be understood from its context, or does it need some qualification to help the reader? (If it does then perhaps it is not the right word.)

JARGON

Jargon is specialised vocabulary, familiar to the members of a group, trade or profession. If you write for a newspaper or general magazine you should try to translate jargon into ordinary English whenever you can. If you write for a specialist magazine there is a stronger case for leaving some terms as they are, but you must be sure that the reader will understand them.

A common source of jargon is scientific, medical, government and legal handouts. Avoid such examples of officialese as:

ambulatory patient	for (one that has been allowed up)
domiciliary unit	(home)
hospitalised	(sent to hospital)

There are also ugly words in industry, but you cannot always avoid them. 'Containerisation', for example, has a precise meaning and is difficult to translate.

'Redundancy' may appear to be a euphemism for sacking – but there is a big difference between the two terms. A person made redundant will not be replaced: their job has been abolished. A person sacked is likely to be replaced.

'Packing' is not the same as 'packaging'; 'marketing' is not the same as 'selling'; 'targeting' may be an ugly word but it is what sales and marketing people say they do when they set out to identify and capture a market. So use these terms where necessary in context but do not use them in general stories.

The computer industry has spawned its own ugly terminology – answer-back, boot up, end-user, formatted, throughput, input, hardware, software. It is apt for that industry since it conveys particular, precise meanings to those who work with computers.

But journalists (except those on computer magazines) should avoid such terms as 'throughput'. We already have words to describe these ideas. They may be less trendy but they are at least as clear as computer jargon and certainly more elegant.

SLANG

'Write as you speak' can be good general advice for trainee journalists. Better by far the vigour and freshness of the spoken word than the dull formality of the official report or the business letter.

But be careful with slang, which could be called the jargon of the street. Similar arguments apply here. Will the reader understand it? Is it ugly? Has the word become accepted?

And does it fit the context? You would not use slang in reporting the mayor's funeral – but you might well use jazz slang in writing a colour piece on Dizzy Gillespie's funeral.

Be particularly careful with rhyming slang which can be euphemistic – as with:

> berk (Berkeley Hunt – cunt)
> bottle (and glass – arse)
> bristols (Bristol Cities – titties)

FOUR-LETTER WORDS . . .

. . . Including of course swear words with more than four letters. Should you use them in copy? And if so, should they be printed in full or muffled by asterisks?

Essentially this is a matter of editorial policy and style. When in doubt, check with your editor or department head.

But it's worth noting that there are far more swear words than there used to be – in journalism as in ordinary conversation. And that tabloids are more likely than broadsheets to protect their readers' sensibilities by asterisks.

WORDS WITH TWO MEANINGS

With some words the problem is that they mean different things to different people. To the history don, for example, a 'chauvinist' is an aggressive patriot, a flag-waver, while to almost anyone under 40 a chauvinist is somebody who puts women down.

Below are some examples of words that can cause confusion. So use them with care – if in doubt, find an alternative.

Note: in most cases the first meaning given is the earlier, 'correct' one, even though the later, looser one may now be more common. (See also *Confusing pairs*, below.)

aggravate: 1 make worse; 2 annoy
alibi: 1 evidence that one was elsewhere when a crime was being committed; 2 excuse
anticipate: 1 use, spend, deal with in advance; 2 expect
arguably: 1 possibly; 2 probably
celibate: 1 unmarried; 2 abstaining from sex
chauvinist: 1 absurdly nationalistic; 2 sexist
chronic: 1 lingering, recurrent; 2 very bad, severe
cleave: 1 split; 2 stick
cohort: 1 group of people (originally military); 2 individual colleague or assistant
contemporary: 1 belonging to the same time; 2 modern
decimate: 1 kill one in ten; 2 kill or destroy large numbers
dilemma: 1 choice between two equally unwelcome possibilities; 2 awkward problem
egregious: 1 distinguished; 2 notorious
fulsome: 1 excessive; 2 copious
gay: 1 light-hearted; 2 homosexual
geriatric: 1 relating to care of the old; 2 old
pristine: 1 original, former; 2 new, fresh, pure
protagonist: 1 chief actor; 2 any participant
refute: 1 show to be false; 2 contradict, deny
regularly: 1 at regular intervals; 2 often

scan: 1 examine closely; 2 glance at (also of verse to conform to rules of metre)
shambles: 1 slaughterhouse; 2 confusion

CONFUSING PAIRS

There are many pairs of words in English that sound similar and are often confused. The pitfall here is not that the two words are thought to have the same meaning but that the unwary writer uses one by mistake for the other – and thus produces an entirely different meaning. In some cases (such as the trio 'assure/ensure/insure') each word has gradually acquired its own distinct meaning: they all mean 'make sure' but in different ways.

See also Chapter 4, *Spelling*, for pairs of words that sound identical and are often confused.

abrogate (abolish)/arrogate (claim presumptiously)
affect (influence, adopt)/effect (as verb, accomplish)
appraise (determine the value of)/apprise (inform)
assure (give confidence to)/ensure (make happen)/insure (arrange insurance)

barbaric (crude, uncivilised)/barbarous (cruel)

censor (prevent publication)/censure (criticise harshly)
chafe (make sore)/chaff (tease)
complacent (smug)/complaisant (obliging)
comprehensive (exhaustive)/comprehensible (intelligible)
contemptible (deserving contempt)/contemptuous (showing contempt)
continual (recurring with breaks)/continuous (without a break)
credible (believable)/credulous (believing too easily)

defective (damaged)/deficient (short of)
definite (precise)/definitive (conclusive)
deprecate (argue or protest against)/depreciate (fall in value)
derisive (showing contempt)/derisory (deserving contempt)
disinterested (impartial)/uninterested (bored)

economic (of economics, enough to give a good return)/economical (thrifty)

elemental (basic)/elementary (simple)
eligible (suitable)/illegible (unclear)
equable (steady)/equitable (fair)
evolve (develop)/devolve (hand down)
exhaustive (comprehensive)/exhausted (tired)
exigent (urgent)/exiguous (scanty)
explicit (stated in detail)/implicit (implied)

farther (used of distance only)/further (used of quantity and distance)
flaunt (display ostentatiously)/flout (treat with contempt)
forceful (energetic)/forcible (done by force)
fortuitous (accidental)/fortunate (lucky)

historic (famous in history)/historical (belonging to history)

imply (suggest)/infer (deduce)
ingenious (cleverly contrived)/ingenuous (frank)
intense (extreme)/intensive (concentrated)

loath/loth (unwilling)/loathe (detest)
luxuriant (profuse)/luxurious (opulent)

masterful (dominating)/masterly (skilful)
militate (contend)/mitigate (soften)

oral (spoken)/verbal (of words, written or spoken)
ordinance (decree)/ordnance (arrangement, usually military)

partly (in part)/partially (incompletely)
politic (prudent)/political (of politics)
practical (opposite of theoretical)/practicable (capable of being done)
prescribe (lay down)/proscribe (prohibit)
prevaricate (evade the truth)/procrastinate (defer action)

repel (offend)/repulse (drive back)

sensual (physical, gratifying to the body)/sensuous (affecting or
    appealing to the senses, especially by beauty or delicacy)

titillate (tease, arouse)/titivate (smarten)

venal (corruptible)/venial (excusable)

REDUNDANT WORDS

Many words used are superfluous, for example adjectives ('*true* facts'), prepositions ('fill *up* a bottle') or phrases ('for *the month of* January'). Often a writer feels the need to add a redundant word or phrase because they do not know the meaning of a particular word. Never do this. Always check what a word means, then decide whether your reader will understand it – without the redundant addition. Here are some examples to avoid:

> **appreciate** *in value*
> *chief* **protagonist**
> *close* **scrutiny**
> *completely* **surround**
> **comprise** *of*
> **consensus** *of opinion*
> **cut** *back*
> *free* **gift**
> *general* **consensus**
> **in** *actual* **fact**
> **revert** *back*
> *temporary* **respite**
> *total* **annihilation**
> *self*-**confessed**

Many redundant expressions trip off the tongue – or can be found in legal documents. But in copy avoid:

> aid and abet
> each and every
> first and foremost
> (without) let or hindrance
> neat and tidy
> null and void
> ways and means

See also *Saying it twice*, p. 26.

NON-EXISTENT WORDS

By all means make up a word if the context demands it. But avoid making up non-existent words by mistake. Do not run together words that belong apart or add syllables to words that do not need them. For example use:

> **a lot** *not* **alot**
> **dissociate** *not* **disassociate**

on to *not* onto
preventive *not* preventative
recur *not* reoccur

But 'alright' is now all right in many publications: check your house style. Also note: 'adaptation' *not* 'adaption'.

EMPTY WORDS

Some words are, simply, empty. 'Simply' used like this is one of them. So is 'basically'. They tend to be used in speech as an alternative to 'er' to give the speaker thinking time. Avoid them in writing unless in quoting somebody you wish to give the impression that they are empty headed. For example:

at the end of the day
basically
by and large
currently
I mean
meaningful
simply
you know
well

AMERICANISMS

American is not a foreign language but a dialect (or series of dialects) of English. And to it we owe much of the vigour of modern English prose. Without writers such as Hemingway our language would be a tired, anaemic thing. American expressions are everywhere. Some enrich the language by saying something previously unsaid or by providing a direct or vivid alternative to the ordinary British expression. The American 'muffler', for example, is a more precise word for 'silencer'.

Others are ugly, clumsy and pointless. Then there are those that make sense to Americans – but if they mean anything at all in Britain, mean something else.

And the position is constantly changing. Yesterday's Americanism, like yesterday's slang, can turn into today's standard English.

Thus British children are increasingly being 'raised' rather than 'brought up': the American expression is shorter, more direct – no problem. But

Britons still ask for a 'rise' in salary rather than a 'raise'. And 'hike', though shorter than 'increase', still suggests fit young people in shorts striding through the countryside.

In British press reports of the 1996 French transport dispute 'truckers' kept appearing. Again, no problem: the word is shorter than 'truck/lorry driver' and clear. But a British headline about 'vets' (for 'army veterans') inspired a reader's letter pointing out that in Britain 'vets' were 'veterinary surgeons'.

And there is a problem about the use of the picturesque American word 'seafood'. Over here it is used to mean either 'shellfish' or 'fish *and* shellfish' – to the gourmand an important distinction.

So be careful in your use of American imports. Above all, avoid those that turn a noun into a verb when a perfectly good verb already exists and those that lengthen an expression without adding to it. For example, do not use:

to consult with	for (to consult)
to gift	(to give)
to loan	(to lend)
transportation	(transport)
utilisation	(use)

But what's the difference between 'envisage' and 'envision', say? Nothing – except that the first is British and the second American. If you work for *Time Out* – a magazine whose title proclaims it as under American influence – there probably won't be a problem. Otherwise there often will be: remember your reader.

CLICHÉS

Everybody who advises on writing in general and journalism in particular says you must avoid clichés. And you must certainly try to avoid the hilarious/embarrassing ones listed below. But a certain amount of formula-writing, both in structure and vocabulary, is inevitable in routine journalism, whether it is a news story or a piece of instructional copy. A worse fault is to try so hard to be original that you end up sounding pretentious.

And there is of course a worse mistake than using a cliché: misusing one. Do not write 'He is as deaf as a doornail' or 'She is as dead as a post.' Avoid mixing two clichés together. Do not write: 'I am full of nothing but praise.' This runs together into a nonsensical cocktail the two stock phrases 'I am full of (praise)' and 'I have nothing but (praise).'

Some common expressions are almost always misused. For example, 'to beg the question' does not mean 'to raise the question' but to avoid the question and so to use as the basis of proof something that itself needs proving. It means arguing in a circle.

A leading question in law is a question put in such a way as to suggest the desired answer. It is helpful rather than hostile.

'The exception proves the rule' means that the exception tests the rule (from the original meaning of 'prove', which also gives us the page proof and that other phrase 'the proof of the pudding is in the eating'), and in law that the making of an exception proves that the rule holds *in cases not excepted*. Thus a notice saying 'Today students may leave early' implies that they usually have to stay late.

The expression cannot mean that an exception to the rule makes it valid.

If you find these definitions difficult to follow – or remember – the best advice may be to avoid the expressions altogether.

If you do use a cliché, don't apologise for doing so by using another one. The following expressions are all lame apologies:

to coin a phrase (always used ironically)
as the saying goes/as the old joke has it
the proverbial . . . (avoid this even if a proverb is quoted)

The following list of clichés appeared in A *Journalist's Guide to the Use of English* published in 1971:

acid test	crying need
any shape or form	
	dame fashion
beggars description	dark horse
bitter end	dastardly deed
blow by blow	dead as a dodo
breakthrough	deaf as a post
bring to a head	denizens of the deep
burning issue	down under
cheer to the echo	each and every
city fathers	extra special
clutches of the law	
cool as a cucumber	face up to

fair means or foul
fair sex
fan the flames
fast and loose
flash in the pan
foregone conclusion

goes without saying
golden handshake
great beyond
grim reaper

high dudgeon
horns of a dilemma

interesting to note

jet-propelled

last but not least
leave no stone unturned
like rats in a trap
limped into port

long years
loom up

monotonous regularity

news leaked out

out and about

pillar of the establishment
pool of blood

red letter day

sea of faces
speculation was rife

take the bull by the horns
theory exploded
this day and age
this point in time
true facts
turned turtle

Every area of journalism has its own set of clichés to be avoided by careful writers and subs. Here, for example, is the *Times Literary Supplement*'s 1997 hitlist of 20 words and phrases to be cut from book reviews:

1 mordant wit
2 If (so-and-so) didn't exist, it/he/she would have to be invented
3 rich tapestry
4 . . . a hilarious and searing indictment of Britain today
5 smorgasbord (of ideas)
6 consummate (as in 'consummate skill')
7 surfing (metaphorically)
8 eponymous (as in 'the eponymous hero')
9 feisty
10 in spite of (or perhaps because of) etc.
11 he/she writes like an angel
12 this curate's egg (of a book)
13 peppered with
14 baggy monster (of a novel)
15 . . . but (such-and-such) looks like carelessness
16 these are mere cavils, minor quibbles etc.
17 (such-and-such/so-and-so) is that rare thing, a . . .
18 made me laugh out loud, couldn't put it down (etc.)

19   having said that . . . arguably . . . (etc.)
20   . . . reminds one of Martin Amis.

MISQUOTATIONS AND MISTAKES

Journalists should know what they are talking about. And when they quote, whether it is the people they interview or the books they read, they should quote accurately. For example, it isn't 'a little knowledge' that is said to be a dangerous thing but 'a little learning'. So also:

Nor all, that *glisters* [not 'glitters'], gold.
To gild refined gold, to *paint* the lily [not 'to gild the lily'].
Till death *us do* [not 'do us'] part.
Water, water everywhere *nor any* [not 'and not a'] drop to drink.

The 'mother of Parliaments' is not the House of Commons but England. And Humphrey Bogart in *Casablanca* never says: 'Play it again, Sam.'

As Bill Bryson has pointed out, the ship whose crew famously disappeared was the *Mary*, not Marie, *Celeste* and Hobson's choice (the horse by the stable door) is not a difficult one but no choice at all.

Frankenstein was not the monster in Mary Shelley's novel but the monster's creator.

Billy the Kid was not left-handed. That belief arose because careless production staff in newspapers flipped his picture, making it look as though he wore his holster on the left.

And finally journalists almost always get the King Canute story wrong. When he told the tide to stop coming in he was not arrogantly expecting it to obey him; by contrast he was showing his courtiers that he was not omnipotent.

Here, as everywhere, the moral is: if you want to be sure, get hold of a reference book and check.

10
Foreign words

There are many foreign words and phrases in current English. As the world's most flexible and widely used language English constantly adopts new words from elsewhere. In particular, the flow of words from French has not stopped since the Norman invasion.

There are also many words and phrases taken from the classical languages, Greek and Latin, still in use. As the classics continue to lose ground in schools, this gives journalists a double problem: first, to become familiar with this vocabulary if they have not previously learnt it; second, to assess how much of it will make sense to their readers.

In certain cases, such as legal terminology, there may be no alternative to using Latin: *habeas corpus*, *sub judice*, *affidavit* can be paraphrased and explained but they remain the precise terms in use. In other cases there is every reason to translate from Latin – or French – into English.

So be careful with words of foreign origin. Use them accurately but not pretentiously, always asking yourself: 'Will my reader understand this?' To put it another way, do not litter your copy with words that would need to be italicised because they are unfamiliar. In general, if a word needs italics, translate it into English.

But if you do use foreign words to spice up your copy, be accurate. Do not follow the *Daily Mail* sub-editor who headlined a story about a French mayor trying to resist the English invasion of his town:

ALLEZ LES ANGLAIS!

Instead of what was meant ('English, go away', which would have been 'Allez-vous-en'), this says the opposite: 'Go on.'

The French word *embonpoint* is not in fact a euphemism for an ample bosom but an everyday word for portliness à la Hercule Poirot. Which makes utter nonsense of this clever-sounding sentence in a *Guardian* sports report:

> The current version of Buster Mathis boasts not just a Michelin-man waist but an *embonpoint* that would give give him a better shot at starring in the next Wonderbra poster than winning a boxing title.

When the Tory politician Alan Clark used the phrase 'economical with the actualité' (as a variant on the original 'economical with the truth') he was making a pretentious blunder: *actualité* means 'topicality' or 'current events'. But this has not stopped the phrase being repeated: it sounds impressive.

An American journalist who interviewed Gérard Depardieu confused the primary meaning in French of *assister à* (to be present at) with its English echo (to help in). As a result the unfortunate French actor (who had grown up in a rough neighbourhood and, as a boy, had *witnessed* a rape) found himself widely accused of being a rapist.

English and French have many *faux amis* – two words from different languages that sound similar but have different meanings. So never guess the meaning of a French word.

Try not to mix the foreign and the English. Say either 'a year' or 'per annum' not 'per year'. (But 'miles per hour/mph' and 'miles per gallon/mpg' are sanctioned by usage.)

If your house style includes accents, make sure that you use them consistently. For example 'paté' and 'emigré' are howlers: they should be *pâté* and *émigré*. And watch your spelling of foreign words: *de rigueur* includes the letter 'u' twice; *restaurateur* has no 'n'; *bête noire* has an 'e' at the end. (For the plurals of foreign words see Chapter 4, *Spelling*, pp. 34–5.)

Below is a selection of foreign words and phrases in current English that you may come across. It is followed by some examples of common classical references. To repeat the point, in both cases use with care.

ab initio: from the beginning (Latin)
actualité: topicality or current events, *not* truth (French)
AD/anno domini: in the year of the lord (Latin)
addendum/a: something to be added, e.g. to a book (Latin)
ad hoc: for this special purpose (Latin), so also adhocery, adhocism, the use of ad hoc measures
ad hominem: personal, used of an argument that attacks the character of an opponent rather than their argument (Latin: 'to the man')

ad infinitum: endlessly (Latin)

ad lib(itum): without restraint, impromptu (Latin: 'according to pleasure')

ad nauseam: to a sickening extent (Latin)

aegis: protection (Greek)

affidavit: written declaration on oath (Latin)

aficionado: fan, originally of bullfighting (Spanish)

à fond: thoroughly, in depth (French)

a fortiori: with stronger reason (Latin)

agent provocateur: person who leads others into committing unlawful acts (French)

agitprop: political propaganda (Russian)

aide-mémoire: reminder, written summary (French)

à la: in the style of – a short form of 'à la mode de': 'à la Hercule Poirot'

à la carte: with the freedom to pick and choose (French)

à la mode: fashionable (French)
(French cookery) of beef – stewed in wine
(American cookery) served with icecream

à la mode de: in the style of (French)

alfresco: in the open air (Italian)

alibi: evidence that one was elsewhere when a crime was being committed (Latin)

alma mater: particular school or university to its students (Latin: 'bounteous mother')

alpha and omega: beginning and end (Greek alphabet)

am/ante meridiem: in the morning (Latin)

amanuensis: literary assistant (Latin)

amen: so be it, agreed (Hebrew)

amour-propre: self-esteem, vanity (French)

anathema: deeply offensive (Greek)

ancien régime: the old system (French: that before the 1789 revolution)

angst: anxiety of a general kind (German)

annus mirabilis: wonderful year (Latin)

Anschluss: take-over, e.g. of Austria by Nazi Germany in 1938 (German: 'union')

ante: fixed stake in poker (Latin: 'before'), hence up/raise the ante – increase costs, demands, etc.

ante-bellum: before the war (Latin), particularly used of the American Civil War

antipasto: first course (Italian: 'before food')

aperçu: insight (French: 'noticed')

apéritif: drink before a meal (French)

apogee: highest point (Greek)

à point: just right (French)

a posteriori: (of reasoning) from effect to cause (Latin)

apparatchik: member of party machine, originally apparat of Communist Party (Russian)

après-ski: fun and games after skiing (French)

a priori: (of reasoning) from cause to effect (Latin)

apropos (of): to the point (French), also used in the opposite sense to mean 'incidentally'

arriviste: ambitious, self-seeking person (French)

à trois: see *ménage*

au contraire: on the contrary (French)

au courant: well-informed (French)

au fait (with): well informed, expert (in) (French)

au fond: fundamentally (French)

au naturel: cooked plainly or served without dressing (French)

au pair: foreign girl who does light domestic work in exchange for room and board (French: 'on equal terms')

au secours: help! (French)

autres temps, autres moeurs: customs change with the times (French)

avant-garde: trend-setting artists, writers, etc. (French)

ave: hail, or farewell (Latin)

bain-marie: pot of boiling water in which another pot is placed to cook slowly (French)

bête noire: bugbear (French)

billet-doux: love letter (French)

bint: derogatory word for girl (Arabic: 'daughter')

blasé: indifferent to pleasure through familiarity (French)

blitz: sudden strong attack (German: 'lightning'), hence the blitzkrieg attack on Poland in 1939

blond(e): fair-haired (French) – see also *Agreement*, p. 37

bona fide: genuine (Latin: 'in good faith'), hence bona fides: genuineness, proof of trustworthiness – *note* bona fides is singular

bonhomie: genial manner (French)

bon mot: witty saying (French)

bonne-bouche: tasty morsel (French)

bon viveur: person who enjoys life, particularly good food (French) *but* in modern French the phrase is 'bon vivant'

boudoir: woman's small private room (French)

bra/brassière: women's undergarment to support the breasts (French) *but* in modern French une brassière is a baby's vest – a bra is 'un soutien-gorge'

branché: switched on, trendy (French)
bric-à-brac: odd items of furniture, ornaments, etc. (French)
brunet(te): dark-haired (French) – see also *Agreement* p. 37

ca/circa: about (Latin)
carpe diem: enjoy the present moment (Latin: 'seize the day')
carte blanche: freedom to do as one thinks (French: 'blank page')
casus belli: cause of/excuse for war (Latin)
caveat: warning (Latin)
caveat emptor: let the buyer beware (Latin)
ceteris paribus: other things being equal (Latin)
cf/confer: compare (Latin)
chaperon(e): older person supervising girl or unmarried woman
    (French) – see also *Agreement*, p. 37
chargé d'affaires: senior diplomat, e.g. ambassador's deputy
    (French)
château: French castle, large country house or wine property
châtelaine: mistress of château (French)
chef d'oeuvre: masterpiece (French)
chutzpah: effrontery, impudence (Yiddish)
cliché: hackneyed phrase or idea (French: 'printing plate')
cogito ergo sum: I think, therefore I am – starting point in
    philosophy of Descartes (Latin)
comme il faut: proper (French)
compos mentis: sane (Latin)
confidant(e): person to confide in (French) – see also *Agreement* p. 37
cons: see *pros and cons*
contra: against (Latin)
coquette: flirt (French)
cordon bleu: (cook) of the highest excellence (French: 'blue ribbon')
cordon sanitaire: isolating barrier (French)
corpus delicti: evidence of a crime, e.g. corpse (Latin)
corrigenda: corrections (Latin)
cortège: funeral procession (French)
cosi fan tutte: what all women do (Italian)
couchette: railway sleeping berth that is convertible by day into
    ordinary seat (French)
coup d'état: sudden overthrow of government especially by force
    (French)
coup de foudre: love at first sight (French: 'thunderbolt')
coup de grâce: death blow (French: 'mercy blow')
coup de main: surprise attack (French) *but* in modern French 'un
    coup de main' is a helping hand
cri de coeur: cry from the heart (French)

crime passionel: crime, e.g. murder, caused by sexual passion
(French)

crise de conscience: crisis of conscience (French)

cui bono?: who stands to gain? (Latin)

cul-de-sac: dead end, blind alley (French: 'bottom of the sack') *but*
in modern French 'voie sans issu' or 'impasse' are far more
common – 'cul' is seen as coarse

culottes: divided skirt (French) *but* in modern French 'une culotte'
(singular) is a pair of panties/underpants

curettage: surgical scraping to remove tissue or growth (French)

cv/curriculum vitae: biographical summary (Latin)

débâcle: sudden disastrous collapse (French)

débutant(e): beginner (French) – see also *Agreement*, p. 37

déclassé: reduced in social standing (French)

décolletage: a low neckline (French)

décolleté: low cut, wearing a low-cut dress (French)

de facto: in fact, actual (Latin)

dégagé: free from constraint, politically uncommitted (French)

De Glanville: like most French surnames starting with 'de', when
anglicised it begins 'De'

déjà vu: feeling that something similar has been experienced before
(French)

de jure: by right (Latin)

de mortuis nil nisi bonum: say nothing but good of the dead
(Latin)

dénouement: resolution of plot (French)

Deo volente: God willing (Latin)

de rigueur: strictly necessary (French)

derrière: euphemism for buttocks (French)

déshabillé: partly dressed (French)

détente: easing of tension between countries (French)

de trop: not wanted, in the way (French: 'excessive')

deus ex machina: contrived solution of plot difficulty in fiction (Latin:
'god from the machinery')

dictum: saying (Latin)

digestif: strongly alcoholic drink after a meal (French)

dishabille: anglicised version of déshabillé – see above

divorcé(e): divorced person (French) – but prefer the anglicised
'divorcee' for both men and women

do/ditto: the same thing (Italian)

dolce far niente: sweet idleness (Italian)

(la) dolce vita: life of luxury (Italian: 'sweet life')

doppelgänger: ghostly double (German: 'double goer')

double entendre: word or phrase with two meanings, one usually indecent (French), *but* in modern French the phrase is 'double entente'

droit du seigneur/jus primae noctis: feudal lord's alleged right to have sex with a vassal's bride on the wedding night (French/Latin)

dulce et decorum est pro patria mori: it is sweet and glorious to die for one's country – Horace (Latin)

dum spiro, spero: while I breathe, I hope (Latin)

éclat: ostentatious brilliance (French)

effluvium: offensive smell (Latin)

eg/exempli gratia: for example (Latin: 'by way of example')

élan: zest and vigour (French)

embonpoint: stoutness, portliness (French: 'in good form') *not* 'ample bosom'

éminence grise: power behind the throne (French: 'grey eminence')

en bloc: all at the same time (French)

entente cordiale: friendly understanding, e.g. between Britain and France in 1904 (French)

ergo: therefore (Latin)

erratum/a: error(s) in writing or printing (Latin)

ersatz: substitute, fake (German)

et al/alii, aliae, alia: and others (Latin)

etc/et cetera: and the rest, and so on (Latin)

ex cathedra: with authority (Latin: 'from the chair of office')

ex gratia: as a favour, not from obligation (Latin)

ex officio: because of one's official position (Latin)

ex parte: from one side only (Latin)

ex post facto: retrospective (Latin)

factotum: servant who does all kinds of work (Latin)

fait accompli: a thing already done, and so irreversible (French)

fakir: religious beggar or ascetic in India (Arabic)

fatwa(h): Muslim sentence of death (Arabic)

faux amis: two similar words from different languages that have different meanings – e.g. the French 'veste' is not a vest but a jacket (French: 'false friends')

faux pas: embarrassing blunder (French: 'false step')

felo de se: suicide (Anglo-Latin: 'felon of himself')

festschrift: celebratory publication (German)

fid def/fidei defensor: defender of the faith (Latin)

floreat: may it flourish (Latin)
frisson: shiver, thrill (French)

Gastarbeiter: migrant worker (German: 'guest worker')
gaucho: South American cowboy; hence 'gauchos', women's knee-length trousers (Spanish)
gaudeamus: let us rejoice (Latin)
gemütlich: cosy (German)
gestalt: organised whole or unit (German)
Gesundheit: good health – to a person who has sneezed (German)
glasnost: Soviet policy of openness launched by Mikhail Gorbachev (Russian)
Götterdämmerung: twilight of the gods (German)
goy: Gentile (Hebrew)
grand guignol: horror drama – from Grand Guignol, a Paris theatre specialising in horror
gringo: Spanish-American for English speaker
gulag: labour camp for political prisoners – from Solzhenitsyn's book *The Gulag Archipelago* (Russian)

habeas corpus: writ requiring that a person be brought before a judge or into court (Latin: 'have the body')
habitué: inhabitant or frequent visitor (French)
hara-kiri: ritual suicide (Japanese)
hoi polloi: derogatory term for the masses (Greek)
hors de combat: out of action (French: 'out of the fight')
hors d'oeuvre: first course (French: 'outside the work')

ibid(em): in the same place (Latin)
idée fixe: obsession (French)
ie/id est: that is to say (Latin)
imbroglio: tangled situation (Italian)
impasse: deadlock (French) – see also *cul-de-sac*
imprimatur: licence to print a book (Latin: 'let it be printed')
in absentia: in one's absence (Latin)
inamorata(o): the beloved (Latin)
in camera: in secret, in a judge's private chambers (Latin: 'in the chamber')
incognito: unknown, in disguise (Italian)
in extremis: at the point of death, in very great difficulties (Latin)
in flagrante delicto: caught in the act (Latin: 'while the crime is burning')
infra dig/dignitatem: beneath one's dignity (Latin)
ingénue: innocent, naive young woman, especially on the stage (French: 'ingenuous')

in loco parentis: in place of a parent (Latin)
in memoriam: in memory of (Latin)
in petto: in secret (Italian)
in situ: in its present or original place (Latin)
inter alia: among other things (Latin)
interim: the meantime, provisional (Latin)
interregnum: period between two reigns (Latin)
Intifada: Palestinian uprising (1987) and continued resistance to Israeli occupation (Arabic)
in toto: entirely (Latin)
in utero: in the womb (Latin)
in vino veritas: truth is told under the influence of alcohol (Latin: 'in wine is truth')
in vitro: in the test tube (Latin)
in vivo: in the living organism (Latin)
iota: very small amount (smallest letter in Greek alphabet)
ipse dixit: dogmatic statement (Latin: 'he himself said it')
ipso facto: by that very fact (Latin)

jawohl: yes indeed (German)
jeu d'esprit: witticism (French)
jus primae noctis: see *droit du seigneur*

kamikaze: suicide attack, originally by Japanese airforce (Japanese: 'divine wind')

laissez/laisser-faire: policy of non-interference (French)
laudator temporis acti: person living in the past (Latin: 'praiser of past times')
Lebensraum: living space, Nazi justification for German expansion (German)
leitmotiv/f: recurring theme (German)
lèse-majesté: treason, affront to dignity (French)
lingua franca: common language used by the people of an area where several languages are spoken (Italian: 'Frankish language')
loc cit/loco citato: in the place just quoted (Latin)
locum (tenens): deputy, substitute (Latin)
locus classicus: best-known or most authoritative passage (Latin)

macho: aggressively male, hence machismo, the cult of this (Spanish)
magnum opus: great work (Latin)
mañana: tomorrow, in the indefinite future (Spanish)

mandamus: writ from higher court (Latin: 'we command')
manqué: having failed, as in 'poet manqué' (French)
maquis: French guerrilla resistance movement
mea culpa: through my own fault (Latin)
mélange: mixture (French)
memento mori: reminder of death (Latin)
ménage à trois: household of three people, each one having a
   sexual relationship with at least one of the others (French)
mens rea: criminal intent (Latin)
mens sana in corpore sano: a healthy mind in a healthy body
   (Latin)
mésalliance: marriage with a social inferior (French)
métier: trade (French)
mirabile dictu: wonderful to relate (Latin)
mo/modus operandi: way of working, e.g. by criminal (Latin)
modus vivendi: arrangement, compromise (Latin: 'way of living')
mot juste: exact word (French)
mutatis mutandis: with necessary changes (Latin)

nb/nota bene: take notice (Latin)
né(e): originally named (French: 'born')
négligée: woman's loose, flimsy dressing gown (French)
nem con/nemine contradicente: without opposition (Latin)
ne plus ultra: the ultimate (Latin)
nihil obstat: permission to print (Latin: 'nothing hinders')
nil desperandum: never despair – Horace (Latin)
nirvana: blissful state (Sanskrit)
nisi: to take effect unless (Latin)
noblesse oblige: rank imposes obligations (French)
noli me tangere: don't touch me (Latin)
nolle prosequi: suspension of legal action (Latin)
nom de plume: pen name, pseudonym (French) *but* the modern
   French phrase is 'nom de guerre'
non compos mentis: not of sound mind (Latin)
non sequitur: conclusion that does not follow from premise(s),
   disconnected remark (Latin)
nostrum: favourite remedy (Latin: 'our own')
nouveau riche: person with newly acquired wealth but lacking in
   refinement (French)

obiter dictum/a: cursory remark(s) (Latin)
objet d'art: small article with artistic value (French)
omnibus: widely comprehensive, origin of 'bus' – large public road
   vehicle (Latin)

op cit/opere citato: in the same book as was mentioned before (Latin)

outré: excessive, eccentric (French), *but* in French it means 'scandalised'

pa/per annum: a year (Latin)

pace: with due deference – used in disagreeing with somebody (Latin)

paean: hymn of praise (Latin)

papabile: (of a prospective pope) electable (Italian)

paparazzo/i: snatch photographer(s) of famous people (Italian)

par excellence: more than all others (French)

pari passu: at an equal rate of progress, simultaneously and equally (Latin)

parti pris: bias, prejudice (French)

passé: past its sell-by date (French)

passim: throughout (Latin)

pax vobiscum: peace be with you (Latin)

peccavi: I have sinned (Latin)

per ardua ad astra: through a steep climb to the stars (Latin)

per capita: a head (Latin)

per cent: for each hundred (Latin)

per contra: by contrast (Latin)

per diem: a day (Latin)

per se: in itself (Latin)

perestroika: restructuring of political and economic system in the Soviet Union of the 1980s

persona (non) grata: acceptable (or not), especially to foreign government (Latin)

petitio principii: begging the question (Latin) – see p. 81

pièce de résistance: the showpiece, especially in a meal (French)

pied-à-terre: second home, usually in city or town (French)

pis aller: makeshift (French)

placet: permission is given (Latin)

pm/post meridiem: afternoon (Latin)

poste restante: post office department where mail is kept until collected (French)

post hoc ergo propter hoc: fallacious argument that A causes B because it is followed by B (Latin)

post-partum: after childbirth (Latin)

pourboire: tip (French)

pour encourager les autres: as an example to others (French)

pp/per pro/per procurationem: by proxy, on behalf of (Latin)

précis: summary (French)

prima facie: at first sight (Latin)

primus inter pares: first among equals (Latin)
pro bono publico: for the public good, used of lawyers working as unpaid volunteers (Latin)
pro-forma: (of an account) official form for completion (Latin)
pro patria: for one's country (Latin)
pro rata: in proportion (Latin)
pros and cons: arguments for and against (Latin)
protégé(e): person under someone's patronage (French)
pro tem(pore): for the time being (Latin)

qed/quod erat demonstrandum: which was to be demonstrated, proved (Latin)
qua: in the capacity of (Latin)
quid pro quo: something given, taken, offered for something else (Latin)
(on the) qui vive: on the alert (French sentry's challenge: 'long live who?')
quondam: former (Latin)
quorum: fixed number of members necessary for a valid meeting (Latin)
qv/quod vide: which see (Latin)

raison d'être: reason for existence (French)
réchauffé: reheated, rehashed (French)
recherché: rare or exotic (French)
recto: front or right-hand page of book (Latin)
reductio ad absurdum: demonstrating the falsity of a proposition by showing that its logical extension is absurd (Latin)
repêchage: extra heat in sporting event giving those eliminated a second chance to go on to the final (French: 'fishing out again')
requiem: Catholic mass, dirge for the dead (Latin)
rigor mortis: stiffening of the body after death (Latin)
RIP/requiescat in pace: may he/she rest in peace (Latin)
roué: dissolute (old) man (French: 'broken on the wheel')

samizdat: underground literature, originally in Soviet Union (Russian)
sans: without (French)
schadenfreude: malicious delight in another's misfortune (German)
sd/sine die: indefinitely (Latin)
semper fidelis: always faithful (Latin)
seq(uens): following (Latin)
seriatim: in succession (Latin)
sic: written here as in the original – used to mark mistakes in quotations (Latin: 'so, thus')

sine qua non: essential condition (Latin)
smörgåsbord: buffet meal of various dishes (Swedish)
soi-disant: self-styled (French)
soigné(e): well-groomed (French)
sotto voce: in an undertone or aside (Italian)
status quo (ante): existing state of things (before change) (Latin)
stet: cancel correction (Latin: 'let it stand')
sub judice: under judicial consideration, so not able to be discussed (Latin)
subpoena: writ commanding attendance (Latin: 'under penalty')
sub rosa: in secrecy, in confidence (Latin: 'under the rose', a symbol of secrecy)
sui generis: the only one of its kind (Latin)
supra: above (Latin)

table d'hôte: fixed price meal (French)
tabla rasa: clean slate (Latin: 'scraped tablet')
Te Deum: hymn of praise and thanksgiving (Latin)
terra firma: dry land or the ground, as opposed to water or sky, originally the mainland as opposed to islands (Latin: 'solid earth')
terra incognita: unknown or unexplored region (Latin)
tête-à-tête: one-to-one, in private (French)
trahison des clercs: betrayal of standards by intellectuals (French)
tricoteuse: French Revolutionary woman who knitted beneath the guillotine (French: 'knitter')
troika: team of three (Russian)
touché: hit acknowledged, in argument as in fencing (French)
tour de force: outstanding performance (French)

Übermensch: superman (German)
ubi supra: where mentioned above (Latin)
uhuru: freedom, national independence (Swahili)
ujamaa: kibbutz-type village community in Tanzania (Swahili)
ult(imo): in the last month (Latin)
ultra vires: beyond one's powers (Latin)

v/vide infra/supra: see (below/above) (Latin)
v/vs/versus: against (Latin)
vade-mecum: pocket reference book (Latin: 'go with me')
vale: farewell (Latin)
verbatim: word for word (Latin)
verboten: forbidden (German)

verb sap/verbum sapienti sat est: no further explanation needed (Latin: 'a word is enough for the wise')

verkramp: narrow-minded, illiberal in apartheid South Africa (Afrikaans)

verlig: enlightened, liberal in apartheid South Africa (Afrikaans)

vice anglais: corporal punishment for sexual gratification, sodomy (French: 'English vice')

victor ludorum: school champion on sports day (Latin)

vieux jeu: old hat (French: 'old game')

virgo intacta: virgin (Latin)

vis-à-vis: in relation to (French: 'face-to-face')

viva (voce): oral exam (Latin)

vivat: long live (Latin)

viz/videlicet: namely (Latin)

vo/verso: back or left-hand page of book (Latin)

volenti non fit injuria: no injury is done to a consenting party (Latin)

volte-face: complete change of attitude (French)

voortrekker: Boer pioneer in South Africa (Afrikaans)

vox pop(uli): public opinion, street interview (Latin: 'voice of the people')

wagon-lit: sleeping car (French)

zeitgeist: spirit of the age (German)

COMMON CLASSICAL REFERENCES

All the examples below might be found in a broadsheet newspaper such as the *Observer* or a weekly review such as the *Spectator*. Some, such as 'aphrodisiac', 'cynic', 'erotic' and 'platonic', are everyday expressions. The problem, as always, is in deciding which ones your reader will recognise and not stumble over.

Whereas most are traditional, one or two have recently acquired new meanings. As sport has become increasingly dominated by money – 'professional' in its worst sense – 'corinthian' is more and more a word of praise for the true amateur. 'Trojan horse' now suggests a covert computer virus as well as a political fifth columnist.

Achilles' heel: a person's weakness – the Greek god Achilles was invulnerable except in the heel

acropolis: citadel, especially that of Athens

Adonis: handsome youth – Aphrodite loved him

Aeneid: Latin epic poem by Virgil; its hero is Aeneas

Amazon: strong, tall, warlike woman – in Greek mythology the Amazons cut off their right breasts to improve their archery

ambrosia: the food and drink of the Greek gods – it gave them everlasting youth and beauty

aphrodisiac: something that arouses sexual desire – from Aphrodite

Aphrodite: beautiful woman, the Greek goddess of love

Apollo: handsome youth, the Greek sun god; hence 'Apollonian', serene, rational (opposite of Dionysian)

Arcadia: mountainous district in Greece where people lived a simple rural life with much music and dancing

Argonaut: adventurer – from the Greeks who sailed with Jason in the Argos in search of the golden fleece

Athene (also Athena): Greek goddess of wisdom; hence Athens, the city, and Athenaeum, a temple of Athene, so a place of learning

Atlas: strong man – the Titan who held up the pillars of the universe

Augean stables: something rotten or corrupt, somewhere in need of a good clean – Hercules did the trick by diverting the river Alpheus through the stables

Augustan age (of literature): classical, refined – taken from that of the Roman emperor Augustus Caesar and applied to 18th-century England

Bacchus: Roman god of wine – hence bacchanals, drunken revels, etc.

Cadmus: see *dragon's teeth*

Caesar: autocrat – from the first Roman emperor, Julius Caesar

caesarian section: delivery of a child by cutting through the abdomen – Julius Caesar was said to have been born this way

Caesar's wife: someone who must be above suspicion

Cassandra: daughter of Priam, King of Troy; she had the gift of prophecy but not the knack of making people believe her; hence 'a prophet of doom who is not heeded' (and a celebrated *Daily Mirror* columnist)

centaur: mythical creature, half-man half-horse

Cerberus: the monster that guarded the entrance to Hades

Charybdis: see *Scylla*

chimerical: imaginary, fanciful – from the chimera, a fire-breathing monster with a lion's head, a goat's body and a serpent's tail

Circe: beautiful sorcerer; hence Circean

corinthian: from Corinth in Greece – in architecture and literary style over-elaborate but in sport showing the spirit of the true amateur: playing the game for its own sake

cornucopia: horn of plenty – a goat's horn overflowing with flowers, fruit and corn

Croesus: King of Lydia and fabulously rich

cross the Rubicon: see *Rubicon*

Cupid: Roman god of love, depicted as a naked boy with wings, bow and arrow; hence Cupid's bow, the upper lip shaped like an archery double bow, and Cupid's dart, the power of love

Cyclops: giant with one eye in the middle of his forehead

cynic: a public pessimist about human motives – from the Cynics, a sect of philosophers founded by Antisthenes of Athens

Daedelus: the Greek artist who constructed the Cretan labyrinth and made wings for his son Icarus and himself

Damocles: was taught the insecurity of happiness by sitting through a feast with a sword hanging over his head – from a single hair

Delphic: difficult to interpret like the oracle of Delphi

Diogenic: cynical, like the Cynic philosopher Diogenes

Dionysian: sensual, abandoned – from Dionysus, the Greek god of wine (opposite of Apollonian)

draconian: extremely severe like the laws of Draco of Athens

dragon's teeth: the teeth of the dragon killed by Cadmus, the founder of Thebes; he sowed them and they turned into armed men who fought among themselves until only five were left

Elysian fields (champs élysées): any delightful place – from Elysium, the home of the blessed after death

Epicurean: person devoted to sensual enjoyment – from Epicurus, the Greek philosopher

Eros: Greek god of love; hence erotic, etc.

Fabian tactics: delaying, cautious – from the Roman general Fabius Cunctator, who saved Rome by wearing down the Carthaginian general Hannibal; hence 'the Fabian Society', formed to encourage the gradual spread of socialist ideas

golden fleece: see *Argonaut*

Gordian knot: intricate knot tied by Gordius, King of Phrygia, and cut by Alexander the Great

Gorgon: one of three female monsters; hence 'an ugly or formidable woman'

Greek gifts: given with intent to harm
Greek god: beautiful man

Hades: the Greek underworld, roamed by the souls of the dead
halcyon days: a time of peace and happiness – from halcyon, the
  kingfisher, once supposed to make a floating nest on the sea,
  thus calming it
harpy: rapacious monster, part-woman part-bird; hence 'a greedy,
  cruel woman'
Heracles: Greek form of Hercules
Hercules: hero of superhuman strength who had to complete the 12
  labours; hence herculean, etc.
Hermes: Greek god of herdsmen, arts, theft and eloquence, the
  messenger of the gods; also identified with the Egyptian god
  Thoth, founder of alchemy, astrology, etc.
hermetic: completely sealed – from Hermes, the Greek name for Thoth
Hippocratic oath: doctor's promise to follow medical code of ethics,
  first drawn up by the Greek physician Hippocrates
Homeric: refers to Homer, the Greek epic poet said to have written
  the Iliad and the Odyssey
hubris: arrogance such as to invite disaster – from Greek tragedy

Icarus: rashly ambitious person – Icarus, son of Daedalus, flew so
  high that the sun melted the wax with which his wings were
  fastened and he fell to his death
Iliad: Greek epic poem, ascribed to Homer, describing the climax of
  the siege of Troy

Janus: Roman two-faced god
Jason: see *Argonaut*
Jove: another name for Jupiter; hence the archaic 'by Jove'
junoesque: large, buxom and beautiful – from Juno, the wife of Jupiter
Jupiter: chief Roman god; the largest planet

labyrinth: maze – the Cretan labyrinth was constructed by Daedalus
  to contain the Minotaur, a bull-headed monster
laconic: terse – from Laconia, whose capital was Sparta
Lethe: river of the underworld causing oblivion to those who drank
  from it
lotus-eater: indolent lover of luxury, one of a people described by Homer as
  eating the fruit of the lotus and living in a state of dreamy forgetfulness
Lucullan: (of a banquet) in the lavish style of the Roman Lucullus

Marathon: scene of a Greek victory over the Persians, from where a messenger ran to Athens to report the good news; thus a long-distance race or other test of endurance

Mars: Roman god of war; the planet next after earth in terms of distance from the sun

Medusa: best known of the three Gorgons, whose head, with snakes for hair, turned observers to stone; hence medusa, the jellyfish

Mercury: Roman god of merchandise, theft and eloquence, the messenger of the gods, and the planet nearest the sun; hence mercurial, lively, volatile (also related to the metal mercury)

Midas: King of Phrygia whose touch turned everything to gold

Mount Olympus: see *Olympus*

Muse: one of the nine daughters of Zeus; thus poetic inspiration

Myrmidon: one of a tribe of warriors who accompanied Achilles to Troy

narcissism: self-obsession – from the Greek youth Narkissos who pined away for love of his own image

nectar: the drink of the gods

Nemesis: the Greek goddess of retribution

Neptune: the Roman sea god and a remote planet of the solar system

nymph: semi-divine spirit inhabiting woods, rivers, etc.; beautiful young woman; hence 'nymphet', a sexually attractive and precocious girl, and 'nymphomania' (of women), insatiable sexual desire

Odyssey: Greek epic poem, ascribed to Homer, describing the wanderings of Odysseus (Ulysses) after the Trojan War; so any long wandering

Oedipus: king of Thebes who unwittingly killed his father and married his mother; hence 'Oedipus complex', describing a son's hostility to his father and intense love of his mother

Olympia: place where the original Olympic games were held

Olympiad: originally the period of four years between Olympic games; now a celebration of the modern games or other international contest

Olympian: godlike person; competitor in games

Olympic games (Olympics): international athletic and other contests held every four years since 1896, a revival of the original Greek games

Olympus: mountain where the Greek gods lived, heaven

Orphean: melodious – from the musician Orpheus whose lyre playing could move inanimate objects

Pan: Greek god of pastures, flocks and woods, worshipped in Arcadia, fond of music

Pandora: the first woman, given a box which she opened to release all the ills of human life

Pantheon: temple of all the gods; complete mythology

Parnassus: Greek mountain sacred to Apollo and the Muses

Parthenon: temple of Athene on the Acropolis in Athens

Parthian shot: arrow fired on the turn by Parthian warrior; hence 'parting shot'

Pegasus: winged horse that sprang from Medusa's blood; hence 'a flight of inspiration or genius'

Periclean: of the Athenian golden age of Pericles

Phaedra complex: difficult relationship between step-parent and son/daughter – from Phaedra who killed herself after being rejected by her stepson

Philippics: three orations by Demosthenes of Athens against Philip of Macedon

platonic: refers to the philosophy of Plato, particularly the idea of love between souls without sexual feeling

Poseidon: the Greek sea god

Priapus: Greek and Roman god of procreation; hence priapic (of men), obsessed with sexuality

Prometheus: he stole fire from heaven so Zeus chained him to a rock

protean: assuming different shapes and sizes – from the Greek sea god Proteus

pyrrhic victory: one achieved at too great a cost as by Pyrrhus, King of Epirus, over the Romans

Rubicon: a stream that marked the boundary between Julius Caesar's province of Cisalpine Gaul and Italy – when he crossed it he effectively declared war on Rome; hence 'to cross the Rubicon' is to take a decisive, irrevocable step

Sapphic: refers to the Greek woman poet Sappho of Lesbos who was said to be homosexual

Saturn: Roman god of agriculture, whose festival in December, the Saturnalia, was the occasion for unrestrained merrymaking; and the planet that was believed to induce a melancholy temperament – hence saturnine, gloomy

satyr: Greek god of the woodlands with tail and long ears, depicted by the Romans as part-goat; a lecherous man

Scylla and Charybdis: two monsters that occupied the two sides of the Straits of Messina between Italy and Sicily; hence 'between

Scylla and Charybdis' means a perilous route in which avoiding one danger brings the traveller closer to the other

siren: fascinating woman, bewitching singer – from the sirens, sea nymphs whose seductive songs lured sailors to their deaths; hence 'a warning signal'

Sisyphean: refers to Sisyphus, King of Corinth, who was condemned to roll a stone up a hill – as it neared the top it would roll down again; hence a laborious and futile task

Socratic: refers to the philosophy and teaching method of the philosopher Socrates – based on asking a series of simple questions

sophistry: specious or fallacious reasoning – from the sophists who taught in Greece

sop to Cerberus: the drugged food given to Cerberus to enable Aeneas to enter Hades; hence 'something to appease', 'a bribe'

Spartacist: follower of Spartacus who led a slave revolt against Rome; hence 'extreme German communist' in 1918 revolution

spartan: tough, austere, militaristic – from the Greek city of Sparta

sphinx: monster in Greek mythology with the head of a woman and the body of a lion which asked travellers riddles – then strangled those that could not solve them; also Egyptian stone figure, particularly the huge enigmatic-looking one near the pyramids at Giza; hence 'a mysterious person or thing'

stentorian: loud, powerful (voice) – from Stentor, a Greek herald in the Iliad

stoic(al): indifferent to pleasure or pain – from the Stoics of Athens

Stygian: black, gloomy – from the Styx, one of the rivers of Hades

sword of Damocles: see *Damocles*

Sybarite: lover of luxury – from Sybaris, a Greek city in ancient Italy

Thebes: name of the capital of both ancient Boeotia in Greece and Upper Egypt

thespian: jocular word for actor – from Thespis, the founder of Greek tragedy

Titan: one of a family of giants, the offspring of Uranus (heaven) and Gaea (earth); hence a person of great strength; also the sun god

triumvirate: rule by three men – originally of Rome by Pompey, Crassus and Caesar

Trojan: solid, dependable, courageous person – from the citizens of Troy

Trojan horse: huge wooden horse in which the Greeks hid to enter the city of Troy; hence fifth columnist and computer program that by subterfuge breaches the security of a system in order to damage it

Ulysses: Latin name for Greek hero Odysseus

Venus: Roman goddess of love and the most brilliant planet
vestal: refers to Roman goddess Vesta; vestal virgins kept the
 sacred fire burning on her altar

wooden horse: see *Trojan horse*

Zeus: the greatest of the Greek gods
zephyr: west wind, especially as personified as a god; soft, gentle
 breeze

11
Figures

Figures are a minefield for journalists. Some find simple arithmetic difficult. Others, having grasped the point of a story involving figures, seem determined to inflict every minor detail on the reader. Journalists often exaggerate the importance of anything, to do with figures and fail to apply their critical faculties to claims based on them.

What cannot be overstated is the need for journalists to be numerate as well as literate. Figures, after all, are facts expressed in numerical terms. If you cannot understand percentages, how can you expect to write an accurate story about them?

If, in 1997, 20 per cent of British people go to the cinema at least once, and in 1998 25 per cent go, that is *not* an increase of 5 per cent. It is an increase of a quarter of 20 per cent – that is, an increase of 25 per cent.

Here I have deliberately gone back a stage from the percentage to the fraction to make the point easier to understand. When writing a story, though, you should not mix different ways of expressing figures – percentages and fractions, say – to make the copy more interesting to read. The effect will be confusion.

If a typical basket of goods costs £1 in year one, £1.10 a year later and £1.20 a year after that, then a retail price index of 100 in year one will be 110 in year two and 120 in year three. The index has risen by 10 points in both years. This is how changes in stock market indexes, where the goods in the basket are shares, are usually reported.

Changes in retail prices tend to be reported in terms of percentage change. For the basket in our example the index has risen by 10 per cent from year one to year two, but the increase from year two to year three is a little under 9.1 per cent – the result of dividing 10p (the increase in price) by £1.10 (the price at the start of the year) and then multiplying by 100. The percentage increase in retail prices is one measure of inflation.

Note that although prices have risen in both years of the example – and by exactly the same cash amount – the rate of inflation has *fallen* in the second year.

Always remember that figures can be interpreted in different ways. Suppose that a survey appears to show that one road accident in four is alcohol-related. In following up the story it may be worth considering the point that – apparently – three accidents in four are *not* alcohol-related.

Be sceptical about polls. Before writing a story based on an opinion poll ask yourself what the questions asked really mean.

All polls based on a sample are subject to what statisticians call a margin of error and other people might call variability in their results. If a poll is repeated, the results will be different each time, even if not a single person changes their views.

In a typical political poll where the real answer is that half the population take a particular view, impeccable pollsters will find that most of the time their results show the figure to be between 47 per cent and 53 per cent with a tendency towards the 50 mark. Thus two polls taken a month apart could report a 6 per cent difference without anybody changing their mind. Similarly, two polls showing a figure of 50 per cent could be describing populations where the true figures were 47 and 53 per cent.

So it makes little sense for journalists to make big stories out of small changes in what the polls are showing.

Even perfectly managed polls will sometimes produce results that lie outside the typical 3 per cent margin of error. This is not an accident: it is exactly what statistics expects. Results like these are often called 'rogue polls'. It is when you get a rogue poll – crying out for sensational treatment because the results are so dramatic – that you need to be most cautious.

Percentage swing is the number of people in a hundred changing sides. If 7 per cent of the population switch from party A to party B, the swing is 7 per cent to party B. Party B's vote goes up 7 per cent and party A's down 7 per cent, so the gap between the parties changes by 14 per cent. That's why it takes only a 7 per cent swing to overturn a 14 per cent majority.

Take care with averages. An average tends to be somewhere in the middle of a set of figures. It is not news to write:

> Almost 50 per cent of British people have shorter than average holidays.

So too with the IQ scale whose midpoint is 100 – about half of us must have an IQ score lower than 100.

Avoid such technical terms as 'mean', 'median' and 'percentile' unless you are writing for a technical journal.

In general, percentages are harder to cope with than fractions – and fractions are harder than whole numbers. So wherever possible say 'one person in 10' rather than '10 per cent' or 'one tenth'.

With money prefer whole figures to decimals – £900,000 not £0.9m – but prefer decimals to fractions. In English decimals take a full point: 12.5. And, except in technical journals, figures greater than 999 take commas: 1,000.

In the house style of most publications figures start at 10 – but avoid mixing figures and words: write '9–10 people' not 'nine–10'.

Never start a sentence – still less a paragraph – with a figure since it looks ugly and creates typographical problems. So instead of:

> '14 people died when . . .'

write:

> 'Fourteen people died when . . .'

Don't solve the problem by writing:

> 'About 14 people died when . . .'

Indeed always avoid approximating precise figures as in:

> 'About 43.3 per cent'/'Around 123 people'

And don't use such phrases as 'a substantial number', 'a significant minority', 'a large proportion', 'a percentage of the population': they are empty words pretending to be precise.

Get dates right. 'Between' must be followed by 'and'; 'from' by 'to'. Do not write 'between 1914–18' or 'from 1914–1918'. Instead write either 'in 1914–18' or 'between 1914 and 1918' or 'from 1914 to 1918'. That makes it possible to write:

> German rearmament took place between 1914–18 and 1939–45.

Should it be first/firstly, second/secondly? The shorter form is preferable but there is nothing wrong with the longer form – check your house style.

The British billion was once worth a million million. Now, as in the United States, it is worth only a thousand million.

Why *the year* 2000 for the millennium? In most cases the phrase is redundant.

Figures are hard to read. Do not litter your copy with them – unless you are writing for a technical journal. Even there, consider taking most of the figures out of the copy and putting them in a box or table.

Finally, do use a calculator to check figures – don't take other people's arithmetic on trust.

12

Broadcast journalism
Harriett Gilbert

The well-behaved Victorian child was supposed to be seen, not heard. Writing for broadcast journalism is the opposite: what matters is not how the words will look but how the listener will hear them.

This can be wonderfully liberating. On the small scale, you can shrug aside such technicalities as the difference between a semicolon and a comma. More importantly, all the preconceived turns of phrase you've absorbed from newspapers, magazines and books can and *must* be chucked away: in writing for broadcast journalism you're returning to the primary language, language as it's spoken, as it's heard.

To begin with, this can pose problems for people used to their words being read. The construction of elegantly complex sentences and the use of long and obscure words can be almost as hard to unlearn as they were to learn. And, if broadcast words when transmitted should sound like conversation, this doesn't mean they should reproduce the mumbles of desultory chat between friends. On the contrary, broadcast English must be vivid and clear.

The first thing to remember is that listeners have only one chance to understand you. Unlike magazine or newspaper readers, they cannot go back to the beginning of a sentence or story. Television sometimes uses graphics to reinforce crucial or complicated points, but viewers are still at the mercy of the medium's forward momentum. Besides, both they and radio listeners are often only half-concentrating.

The second thing to remember is the power of the voice. Whereas writers for print must rely on their words alone for colour, inflection, emphasis, broadcast journalists have the use of their own or somebody else's voice. Television, of course, uses pictures as well – in a different, more integrated and extensive way than the print media – but the voice is nonetheless an important component of all broadcast journalism. Your writing should therefore serve the voice as much as the voice serves your writing.

This chapter examines the implications of these two points for the broadcast journalist.

MAKING THINGS EASY FOR THE NEWSREADER OR PRESENTER

There is one person who will be treating what you write as a visual object – either yourself, when you're seated with your script before the microphone, or the newsreader or presenter who must bring your script to life.

SPELLING

It is sometimes said that broadcast journalists may ignore the rules of spelling. Up to a point this is so. The listener, after all, would be blithely unaware that you had spelt 'Carribean' thus, while a newsreader who spotted the mistake would be unlikely to be thrown.

Unlikely to be, but not incapable of being: the smallest mistake can throw a reader's concentration (even when the reader is the writer who made the mistake in the first place), causing a 'fluff' if not at the time then a few words later on. For this reason, if for no other, the rules of spelling should be observed.

The one occasion on which it makes sense to spell a word incorrectly is when there is likely to be a pronunciation problem. Foreign names, especially, are often better spelt phonetically: 'the Hollywood actress LOUISE RINER (Luise Rainer)', etc. If a script contains such problems, a writer will often warn the reader at the top of the page.

PUNCTUATION – AND OTHER MARKS

In print journalism, punctuation usually follows certain formal rules, rules which help the reader disentangle the meaning of a complicated sentence. In broadcast journalism there should never be a complicated sentence (see below). Punctuation in a script for broadcast is there for one purpose only: to show that there should be a pause between one group of words and another.

As a rule the shortest type of pause is shown by a comma; a slightly longer one by a dash or an ellipsis (three dots); a longer one still by a full stop plus several spaces (not just one, as is now the convention when writing for print); and the longest of all, for a total change of subject or idea, a full stop plus a new paragraph. The important thing is to create spaces that the newsreader or presenter can clearly see arriving, not to fiddle around with colons and semicolons.

Punctuation aside, a whole range of marks may be used by writers, presenters or newsreaders. Important words, especially names, are often put in capital letters; words may be underlined to show that they should be stressed; some people draw little curved arrows to suggest upward or downward inflection, or hyphenate words that should run together in one sense-block, or write in brackets the kind of instruction more usually associated with play scripts: '(SMILE)'. The important thing is that any mark should help the reader communicate in a clear and lively manner.

Of all these marks, perhaps the most useful are those that show that something should be stressed; presenters and newsreaders often make such marks before they go on air. In every phrase, for instance, there is usually one crucial word – 'Top temperature this evening, a sticky nineteen . . .' Underlining it prevents the reader from stressing something less appropriate – a sticky nineteen . . . – an easy mistake to make when inexperienced or preoccupied. Similarly, where individual words need the stress on a contentious syllable – the BBC likes 'controversy' to be pronounced 'controversy' – the reader might make an appropriate underlining.

ABBREVIATIONS

Newspaper readers would have no problem with the following: 'The Bishop of London, the Rt Rev Richard Chartres, has announced . . .'. Even those who didn't automatically translate the abbreviation into 'Right Reverend' would understand enough of its meaning to go on. But a radio or television newsreader, however informed about church titles, would be forced to switch from one kind of thinking to another, opening a gap for a hesitation at the least.

Apart from the most common examples, Mr, Ms, Dr – which the brain recognises more quickly than it would the spelt-out words – abbreviations should be avoided when writing for broadcast journalism. This applies not only to titles but to dates, large numbers, anything which needs mental gymnastics to translate its meaning into sounds. So:

The 10th of January *not* 10 Jan

Five hundred thousand *not* 500,000

MAKING THINGS EASY FOR THE LISTENER

When writing for broadcast it is important to understand how your words will be heard. The person watching television is often also doing something else; the radio listener is almost certainly buttering his children's breakfast toast, shaving her underarms in the bath or negotiating the rush hour. You need to write as though you were addressing a distracted casual acquaintance.

THE LISTENER

I say 'casual acquaintance' in the singular because it is more than likely that your words will be heard by a person on their own. Except in cases of national emergency, people no longer sit round the radio in a group – while even television viewers are often alone in front of the set. Thus, although the broadcast media reach more people than the print media, you should always write for one person. Not 'Some of you may have heard . . .' but 'You may have heard . . .'.

WORDS

Choose unambiguous, straightforward, everyday words: 'death' rather than 'demise'; 'help' rather than 'assist'.

And be on your guard against aural ambiguities, the most notorious of which occurred during a test match when cricket commentator Brian Johnston told the world:

'The batsman's Holding. The bowler's Willey.'

SENTENCE STRUCTURE

Keep sentences short and simple. A sentence riddled with subclauses might be all right in print:

> Khmer Rouge guerrillas kidnapped Christopher Howes, a mine-clearing expert and veteran of Northern Ireland, the Falklands and Iraq, and his interpreter, Houn Hourth, 13 months ago while they were working near the Angkor temples in the north west of the country.

For broadcast, the information would be better split up like this:

> Khmer Rouge guerrillas kidnapped Christopher Howes and his interpreter, Houn Hourth, 13 months ago. The two men were working near the Angkor temples in the north west of the country. Howes is a mine-clearing expert and veteran of Northern Ireland, the Falklands and Iraq.

Even in short sentences, avoid inverted constructions in which a subclause comes before the main clause. For print, where readers have the whole sentence in front of them, the following may be acceptable:

> Because of medical ignorance, thousands of men suffering from prostate cancer are undergoing unnecessary operations.

For broadcast news, where listeners at first don't know what's coming, and then it's gone, the following would be more helpful:

> Thousands of men suffering from prostate cancer are undergoing unnecessary operations because of medical ignorance.

And although, for print, there's a rule of thumb that the most important words should come first, for broadcast journalism the rules are slightly different: your listener may not always catch the very first words of an item, so beginning with the most important words is self-defeating. Instead of:

> Two people have died in a fire in South London . . .

it would be more effective to write:

> A fire in South London has claimed two lives . . .

Equally – unlike in print, where news stories tend to dwindle out, on the basis that only the committed reader will have bothered to follow through to the end – in broadcast news the listener, who isn't able to move on at will, needs to be given a strong ending. The last sentence should not only round the story off but keep its strongest word for the end. Not:

> The woman would have been rejected for in-vitro fertilisation had they known what her true age was.

But:

> If they'd known her true age, the woman's request for in-vitro fertilisation would've been rejected.

QUOTES AND ATTRIBUTION

Because quotation marks aren't audible, it's better to use reported speech than to run the risk of someone's opinion being heard either as fact or as the broadcaster's opinion. The following is clear when you can see it:

> One British Museum insider said staff were never searched when leaving. 'We all know objects routinely disappear as souvenirs. Most losses are not noticed, never mind reported.'

For broadcast, it would be clearer to write:

> One British Museum insider said staff were never searched when leaving. He added that everyone knew objects routinely disappeared as souvenirs but that most losses weren't noticed, never mind reported.

ADJECTIVES

Strings of adjectives don't work on air – and, besides, are largely made redundant by the power of the broadcaster's voice to convey such colours as horror, sadness, joy, irony, amusement and so on.

SIGNPOSTING

In print, such visual devices as new paragraphs or blobs/bullet points can show the reader that the story is changing tack. For listeners, it is helpful to signpost such changes with words:

> Let's look at the implications . . . To summarise the main points . . . But what led up to this situation?

Remember always that you are leading your listeners along a path and that, if you want them to stay with you, they must never feel that they're lost.

INFORMALITY

News writing is usually more formal than writing for a magazine programme, a feature or a traffic up-date, but in all cases it is usual to write 'hasn't' instead of 'has not', for example, or even 'shouldn't've' instead of 'should not have'. Similarly, it is more appropriate to write 'Tony Bullimore, who's 58, was rescued . . .' than: 'Tony Bullimore, 58, was rescued . . .'. The latter works visually but sounds odd (try it).

GRAMMATICAL CORRECTNESS

Informality is not, however, the same as grammatical barbarism. In writing for broadcast there is no good reason to use 'less' when you mean 'fewer' or to describe something as 'different to' something else, instead of 'different from'. Your listeners and viewers are no less educated than magazine and newspaper readers – and are just as likely to be irritated (and distracted) by errors of grammar.

The only occasions on which it is right to break the rules of English grammar are those when *not* to do so would distract your listeners. If, for instance, using 'whom' correctly would sound strange and pompous to your listeners, then drop it in favour of an incorrect 'who'. What matters most is whether the listeners to the station for which you are writing would be more distracted by, for example, 'for whom she was waiting . . .' or 'who she was waiting for . . .'.

READ YOUR WRITING OUT LOUD

Perhaps the most important rule for writers of broadcast journalism is that you should always check your script by reading it out loud. Not inside your head, but vocally: actually *voicing* the sentences as you write them, and when you've written them – partly to check for tongue twisters, ambiguities, double entendres, but also to ensure that the words sound as though they might reasonably be *said*.

All over the country, radio stations are dotted with writers talking to themselves at the keyboard, or standing in corridors reading their scripts with eyebrows shooting all over the place and faces twisted into grimaces. If you can bring yourself to look that ridiculous, you'll produce a script in which there is nothing that might cause a reader to stumble; whose words are straightforward, everyday ones; whose sentences are short and unambiguous; whose switches of thought, direction or subject are signposted; and which provides a sound basic outline for the newsreader or the presenter to colour with the palette of their voice. In short, you will have written a good script for broadcast.

Glossary of terms used in journalism

ABC: Audit Bureau of Circulation – source of circulation figures
advertorial: advertisement presented as editorial
agony aunt: advice giver on personal problems sent in by readers
artwork: illustrations accompanying copy
ascender: portion of lower-case letter that sticks out above the x-height
attribution: identifying source of information or quote

back bench (the): senior newspaper journalists who make key production decisions
backgrounder: explanatory feature to accompany news story
banner (headline): one in large type across front page
bill: poster promoting newspaper, usually highlighting main news story
bleed: (of an image) go beyond the type area to the edge of the page
blob par: paragraph introduced by blob/bullet point
blurb: another name for standfirst or similar displayed copy
body type: the main typeface in which a story is set
bold: thick black type use for emphasis
breaker: typographical device, such as crosshead, to break up text on the page
broadsheet: large-format newspaper such as the Times
bust (to): (of a headline) be too long for the space available
byline: name of journalist who has written the story

calls: routine phone calls by reporters to organisations such as police and fire brigade
caps: capital letters
cast off (to): estimate length of copy

catchline: single word identifying story typed top right on every page

centre (to): set (headline) with equal space on either side

centre spread: middle opening of tabloid or magazine

chapel: office branch of media union

character: unit of measurement for type including letters, figures, punctuation marks and spaces

chequebook journalism: paying large sums for stories

chief sub: senior journalist in charge of sub-editors

city desk: financial section of British newspaper (US: home news desk)

clippings/clips: press cuttings

colour piece: news story written as feature with emphasis on journalist's reactions

contacts book: a journalist's list of contacts with their phone numbers

copy: text of story

crop (to): cut (image) to size

crosshead: occasional line(s) of type usually bigger and bolder than body type, inserted between paragraphs to liven up page

cut-out: illustration with background masked or cut to make it stand out on the page

cuts: press cuttings

dateline: place from which copy is filed, usually abroad

deadline: time by which a journalist must complete story

deck: one of series of headlines stacked on top of each other

delayed drop: device in news story of delaying important facts for effect

descender: portion of lower-case letter that sticks out below the x-height

deskman: American term for male sub-editor

diary (the): list of news events to be covered; hence an off-diary story is one originated by the reporter

diary column: gossip column

direct input: transmission of copy direct from the journalist's keyboard to the computer for typesetting (as opposed to the old system in which printers retyped copy)

display type: type for headlines, etc.

doorstepping: reporters lying in wait for (usually) celebrities outside their homes

double spread: two facing pages

downtable (subs): those other than the chief sub and deputies

dummy: 1 photocopied or printed (but not distributed) version of new publication used for practice and discussion; 2 blank version of established publication, for example, to show weight of paper; 3 complete set of page proofs

edition: version of newspaper printed for particular circulation area or time

editorial: 1 leading article expressing publication's opinion; 2 matter that is not advertising

em, en: units of measurement for type – the width of the two letters m and n

embargo: time before which an organisation supplying material, e.g. by press release, does not want it published

exclusive: claim by newspaper or magazine that it has a story nobody else has

face: type design

feature: article that goes beyond reporting of facts to explain and/or entertain

file (to): transmit copy

fireman: reporter sent to trouble spot when story breaks

flatplan: page-by-page plan of magazine issue

flush left or right: (of type) have one consistent margin with the other ragged

fount (pronounced 'font' and sometimes spelt that way): typeface

free: free newspaper

freebie: something useful or pleasant, often a trip, supplied free to journalists

freelance: self-employed journalist who sells material to various media

freelancer: American term for freelance

full out: (of type) not indented

galley proof: typeset proof not yet made up into a page

gutter: space between pages in centre spread

hack/hackette: jocular terms for journalist

hanging indent: set copy with first line of each paragraph full out and subsequent lines indented

heavy: broadsheet newspaper

house style: *see* Chapter 7

imprint: name and address of publisher and printer
indent: set copy several characters in from left-hand margin
in-house: inside a media organisation
input (to): type copy into computer
insert: extra copy to be included in existing story
intro: first paragraph of story
italics: italic (sloping) type

journo: jocular term for journalist
justified: type set with consistent margins

kill (to): to drop a story; hence 'kill fee' for freelance whose commissioned story is not used
knocking copy: story written with negative angle

layout: arrangement of body type, headlines and illustrations on the page
leader: leading article expressing publication's opinion
leading (pronounced 'ledding'): space between lines (originally made by inserting blank slugs of lead between lines of type)
leg: column of typeset copy
legal (to): check for legal problems such as libel
lensman: American term for male photographer
lift (to): steal a story from another media outlet and reproduce it with few changes
linage (this spelling preferred to lineage): payment to freelances by the line
listings: lists of entertainment and other events with basic details
literal: typographical error
lobby (the): specialist group of political reporters covering the House of Commons
lower case: ordinary letters (not caps)

make-up: assembly of type and illustrations on the page ready for printing
masthead: newspaper's front-page title
must: copy that must appear, e.g. apology or correction

newsman: American term for male reporter

nib: news in brief – short news item
night lawyer: barrister who reads proofs for legal problems

obit: obituary
off-diary: see diary (the)
off-the-record: statements made to a journalist on the understanding that they will not be reported directly or attributed
on spec: uncommissioned (material submitted by freelance)
on-the-record: statements made to a journalist that can be reported
and attributed
op-ed: feature page facing page with leading articles

page proof: proof of a made-up page
par/para: paragraph
paparazzo/i: photographer(s) specialising in pursuing celebrities
paste-up: page layout pasted into position
pay-off: final twist or flourish in the last paragraph of a story
pic/pix: press photograph(s)
pica: unit of type measurement
pick-up (of photographs): those that already exist, which can
therefore be picked up by journalists covering a story
piece: article
point: 1 full stop; 2 standard unit of type size
proofread (to): check proofs
pull-out quotes: short extracts from feature set in larger type as
part of page layout
pyramid (usually inverted): conventional structure for news story with
most important facts in intro

query: question mark
quote: verbatim quotation
quotes: quotation marks

range left or right: (of type) have one consistent margin with the
other ragged
reverse out: reversal of black and white areas of printed image
roman: plain upright type
RSI: repetitive strain injury attributed to over-use and misuse of
computer keyboard, mouse, etc.
run on: (of type) continue from one line, column or page to the next

running story: one that is constantly developing, over a newspaper's
different editions or a number of days

sanserif: plain type
scoop: jocular word for exclusive
screamer: exclamation mark
sell: another name for standfirst, often used in women's magazines
serif: decorative addition to type
setting: copy set in type
shy: (of headline) too short for the space available
side-head: subsidiary heading
sketch: light-hearted account of events, especially parliamentary
slip: newspaper edition for particular area or event
snap: early summary by news agency of important story to come
snapper: jocular term for press photographer
snaps: press photographs
spike: where rejected copy goes
splash: tabloid's main front-page story
splash sub: sub responsible for tabloid's front page
spoiler: attempt by newspaper to reduce impact of rival's exclusive
by publishing similar story
standfirst: introductory matter, particularly used with features
stet: ignore deletion (Latin for 'let it stand')
stone sub: sub-editor who makes final corrections and cuts on page
proofs
story: article, especially news report
strap(line): introductory words above main headline
Street (the): Fleet Street, where many newspapers once had their
offices
stringer: freelance on contract to a news organisation
sub: sub-editor – journalist who checks, corrects, rewrites copy, writes
headlines, captions, etc., and checks proofs; on newspapers, but
not on most magazines, subs are also responsible for layout

tabloid: popular small-format newspaper such as the Sun
taster: production journalist who checks and selects copy
think piece: feature written to show and provoke thought
tip: information supplied, and usually paid for, whether by freelance
or member of the public
tot: triumph over tragedy, feature formula particularly popular in
women's magazines
typo: American term for typographical error

underscore: underline
upper case: capital letters

vox pop: series of street interviews (Latin: 'vox populi' – voice of the people)
widow: line of type consisting of a single word or syllable
wob: white on black – type reversed out

x-height: height of the lower-case letters of a typeface (excluding ascenders and descenders)

Further reading*

JOURNALISM

Although the famous Harold Evans series is out of print, there are books available on most aspects of British journalism. Waterhouse is particularly well written and fun to read, and Spiegl is a laugh a line. Although it has a specialist title, Albert's book makes many useful general points.

Aitchison, James, *Writing for the Press*, Hutchinson, 1988.

Albert, Tim, *Medical Journalism*, Radcliffe Medical Press, 1992.

Bagnall, Nicholas, *Newspaper Language*, Butterworth/Heinemann, 1993.

Boyd, Andrew, *Broadcast Journalism*, Butterworth/Heinemann, 1993.

Bromley, Michael, *(Teach Yourself) Journalism*, Hodder & Stoughton, 1994.

Chantler, Paul, and Harris, Sam, *Local Radio Journalism*, Butterworth/ Heinemann, 1993.

Clayton, Joan, *Journalism for Beginners*, Piatkus, 1992.

—— *Interviewing for Journalists*, Piatkus, 1994.

Davis, Anthony, *Magazine Journalism Today*, Butterworth/Heinemann, 1988.

Dick, Jill, *Freelance Writing for Newspapers*, A. & C. Black, 1991.

Dobson, Christopher, *Freelance Journalism*, Butterworth/Heinemann, 1992.

Evans, Harold, *Newsman's English*, Heinemann, 1972, out of print. (Also by Evans in the same series: *Handling Newspaper Text*, *News Headlines*, *Picture Editing*, *Newspaper Design*, all published in 1972; all out of print.)

Giles, Vic, and Hodgson, Frank, *Creative Newspaper Design*, Butterworth/ Heinemann, 1990.

* Dates refer to the most recent known edition

Goldie, Fay, *Successful Freelance Journalism*, Oxford University Press, 1985.

Greenwood, Walter, and Welsh, Tom, *McNae's Essential Law for Journalists*, Butterworth, 1992.

Harris, Geoffrey, and Spark, David, *Practical Newspaper Reporting*, Butterworth/Heinemann, 1993.

Henessy, Brendan, *Writing Feature Articles*, Butterworth/Heinemann, 1993.

Hodgson, Frank, *Subediting: Newspaper Editing and Production*, Butterworth/Heinemann, 1987.

—— *Modern Newspaper Practice*, Butterworth/Heinemann, 1992.

Hoffman, Ann, *Research for Writers*, A. & C. Black, 1992.

Hutt, Alan, and James, Bob, *Newspaper Design Today*, Lund Humphries, 1988.

Jones, Graham, *Business of Freelancing*, BFP Books, 1987.

Keeble, Richard, *The Newspapers Handbook*, Routledge, 1994.

Keene, M., *Practical Photojournalism*, Butterworth/Heinemann, 1993.

Moore, Chris, *Freelance Writing*, Hale, 1996.

Niblock, Sarah, *Inside Journalism*, Blueprint, 1996.

Sellers, Leslie, *The Simple Subs Book*, 2nd edn, Pergamon, 1985.

Spiegl, Fritz, *Keep Taking the Tabloids*, Pan, 1983, out of print.

—— *Media Speak/Media Write*, Elm Tree Books, 1989.

Waterhouse, Keith, *Waterhouse on Newspaper Style* (replaces *Daily Mirror Style*, now out of print), Viking, 1989.

Wilby, Peter, and Conroy, Andy, *The Radio Handbook*, Routledge, 1994.

Wilson, John, *Understanding Journalism*, Routledge, 1996.

ENGLISH USAGE AND STYLE

THE CLASSICS

On usage the standard texts are Fowler and Gowers; on style Quiller-Couch and Middleton Murry. There is also a famous essay by George Orwell and an American gem, Strunk and White.

Burchfield, Robert, *The New Fowler's Modern English Usage*, Clarendon, 1996.

Fowler, H. W., *The King's English*, Oxford University Press, 1931.

Gowers, Ernest, *The Complete Plain Words*, revised by Bruce Fraser, Penguin, 1987.

Murry, J. Middleton, *The Problem of Style*, Oxford University Press, 1922, out of print.

Orwell, George, 'Politics and the English Language', in Sonia Orwell and Ian Angus, eds, *Collected Essays, Journalism and Letters of George Orwell*, vol. IV, Penguin, 1970.

Quiller-Couch, Arthur, *On the Art of Writing*, Cambridge University Press, 1919, out of print.

Strunk, William, and White, E. B., *The Elements of Style*, New York: Macmillan, 1979.

THE MODERNS

Many of the books listed below are by journalists. Particularly recommended are Bryson and Phythian (a distinguished schoolteacher). Lanham is a spirited attack on the classics.

Aitchison, James, *Dictionary of English Grammar*, Cassell, 1996.

—— *Guide to Written English*, Cassell, 1996.

Blamires, Harry, *Correcting Your English*, Bloomsbury, 1996.

Bryson, Bill, *The Penguin Dictionary of Troublesome Words*, Penguin, 1984.

Crystal, David, *Who Cares about English Usage?*, Pelican, 1984.

Dummett, Michael, *Grammar and Style for Examination Candidates and Others*, Duckworth, 1993.

Fieldhouse, Harry, *Everyman's Good English Guide*, Dent, 1982, out of print.

Greenbaum, Sidney, and Whitcut, Janet, *Longman Guide to English Usage*, Penguin, 1996.

Lanham, Richard A., *Style: An Anti-Textbook*, Yale University Press, 1973.

Partridge, Eric, *Usage and Abusage*, Penguin, 1973.

Phythian, B. A., *Concise Dictionary of Correct English* (replaces *Teach Yourself Good English* and *Teach Yourself Correct English*), Hodder & Stoughton, 1993.

Silverlight, John, *Words*, Macmillan, 1985, out of print.

Vallins, G. H., *Good English, Better English, The Best English*, Pan, 1963, out of print.

Waterhouse, Keith, *English Our English*, Viking, 1991.

Weiner, E. S. C., and Hawkins, J. M., *The Oxford Guide to the English Language*, Oxford University Press, 1984.

Whale, John, *Put It In Writing*, Dent, 1984.

Wood, F. T., Flavell, R. H., and Flavell, L. M., *Current English Usage*, Macmillan, 1981.

PUNCTUATION

Carey, G. V., *Mind the Stop*, Penguin, 1971.
Clark, John, *English Punctuation and Hyphenation*, Harrap, 1990.
Partridge, Eric, *You Have a Point There*, Routledge, 1990.

HOUSE STYLE

Bryson, Bill, *Penguin Dictionary for Writers and Editors*, Viking, 1991.
Grimond, Joe, *The Economist Pocket Style Book*, Business Books, 1991.
Inman, Colin, *The Financial Times Style Guide*, Pitman, 1994.
Jenkins, Simon, ed., *Times Guide to English Style and Usage*, Times Books, 1992.
Macdowall, Ian (comp.), *Reuters Handbook for Journalists*, Butterworth/Heinemann, 1992.
The Oxford Dictionary for Writers and Editors, Oxford University Press, 1981.
The Oxford Writers' Dictionary (paperback version of *The Oxford Dictionary for Writers and Editors*), Oxford University Press, 1990.

DICTIONARIES AND THESAURUSES

Every journalist needs a good dictionary. Of those published by the four main publishers, Oxford University Press, Collins, Longmans and Chambers, the Chambers series is particularly popular among journalists.

A thesaurus can help you write headlines; its disadvantage is that it tends to blur distinctions between words. But there is a reference book that overcomes this disadvantage by combining the functions of dictionary and thesaurus:

Collins Concise Dictionary and Thesaurus, Collins, 1991.

Also note this neat combination:

Weiner, E. S. C., and Waite, Maurice, *The Oxford Dictionary and English Usage Guide*, Oxford University Press, 1996.

DEVELOPMENT OF ENGLISH

The most erudite book is by Burchfield, formerly chief editor of the *Oxford English Dictionary*. Honey's, subtitled '*The Story of Standard English and its Enemies*', attacks the trendy academics. The others are all worth reading. Howard, literary editor of *The Times*, has written several other books on English.

Bryson, Bill, *Mother Tongue*, Hamish Hamilton, 1990.
Burchfield, Robert, *The English Language*, Oxford University Press, 1986.
Crystal, David, *The English Language*, Pelican, 1990.
Honey, John, *Language is Power*, Faber, 1977.
Howard, Philip, *The State of the Language*, Penguin, 1986.
McCrum, Robert, MacNeil, Robert, and Cran, William, *The Story of English*, Faber, 1992.
Potter, Simeon, *Our Language*, Penguin, 1990.

Index